THE TAMING
A TEACHER SPEAKS

THE TAMING

A TEACHER SPEAKS

Deborah James

McGRAW-HILL BOOK COMPANY
NEW YORK, ST. LOUIS, SAN FRANCISCO
TORONTO, LONDON, SYDNEY

ILLUSTRATIONS BY ARNO STERNGLASS

THE TAMING
A TEACHER SPEAKS

Library of Congress Catalog Card Number 68-27508

1   2   3   4   5   6   7   8   9   0   V   B   V   B

7   5   4   3   2   1   0   6   9   8

TO DR. ROBERT SHELLOW

This work was originally undertaken under the auspices of the Special Projects Section of the Mental Health Study Center of the National Institute of Mental Health.

PREFACE

So you want to be a teacher? That's great. Undoubtedly you have recognized the importance of teaching to society and are reaching for the rich human relations possible in this profession. But have you explored the conditions which exist in a classroom?

"Sure," you might reply. "I went to public schools twelve years before I came to college. I know a lot about schools." This is true, but until you've taught, you know very little about what a school is like to the teacher. Neither, just because you've been a child in a family all your life, do you know what it's like to be a father or a mother. A teacher finds a school quite a different place when he returns with a grade book under his arm and a red, ball-point pen clutched firmly in his fist.

This book is designed to help you prepare for the conditions you will meet when you enter the school as a teacher. Many views of our school system have been given in recent times, but generally teachers are too busy to take time to give a teacher's view. Frustrated with my own inadequacies and those of the system in which I taught, I resigned from teaching and took time to sit down and describe for someone not familiar with the system the school in which I had taught for ten years, a suburban high school in a metropolitan area. The school grew from 1,700 to 2,700 students in the decade I taught and was in a community which was neither rich nor poor, typical of the solid middle class. Rather than broad, my experience has been deep. I was helping to develop a curriculum called "psychology" in a school which was part of the community in which I lived. As you walk through these halls and classrooms with me, you will realize as I do that some of these experiences are common to most schools and that some are unique. As you grow in teaching experience, you will need to decide for yourself which is which.

Today the school is the father of our youth. Changes in our society have gradually and continually given a greater burden to the school in shaping the individual. As parents have become more loving and less demanding of their children, the school has become the stern parent, requiring the individual to conform and to measure up to the standards set by our society. It is the school that does the taming. Forced by law and custom to attend school for many years of their lives whether or not they have any desire to learn, many of the students in our schools feel trapped as, indeed, they are.

As the writing of this book progressed, I became aware of the basic power of the system, which was impossible to see in the midst of the confusion and pressure which constitute a teacher's life. I hope this view will help you to find greater depth in your teaching experience and to maintain the elements in the system which are strong in the midst of the change our schools are facing.

Deborah James

CONTENTS

THE TAMING
A TEACHER SPEAKS

CHAPTER ONE

The Cage

THE PHYSICAL PLANT

"I believe a classroom can be compared to a cage in
the zoo. There are about 30 individual species
who are held in one cage for about an hour. During
this hour, as in the zoo, there are visitors who come
and peer through the window and try to see how
many of the species they can get to smile or laugh,"
writes Darla White, a senior.

The physical plant is good. While showing a guest from Indochina around the school last year, I began to realize through his eyes what an excellent job our country has done in providing for the material needs of education. One tends to take for granted these facilities as one becomes accustomed to them. As he was marveling at the cafeteria which competently serves 1,000 students in thirty minutes with a noise level that permits individual conversation, I was thinking about the rule that we could not hang anything from the ceiling to decorate for proms because of the same acoustical tile that he was admiring.

The plant is efficient in much the same way that America is efficient: Material needs are satisfied. The school is big—long, low, and narrow. Only two stories high, it covers a city block across the front with three wings going back at right angles. This E-shaped construction, in which each section consists of two rows of classrooms separated by a hall, provides each classroom with an outside row of windows. The new wing is an exception because it is air-conditioned and theoretically needs no windows.

The architectural design lacks beauty. It is purely utilitarian, and no effort has been made to soften or vary the austere lines. The solid brick structure is neat and efficient, but not aesthetic. After ten years and some feeble effort by the parent-teacher association to landscape the grounds, the view from the outside continues to be one of unrelieved monotony. Parking lots surround the school, and a double road separated by a fence fronts the school. This fence marks the boundary line of the school property. Since it is against regulations for students to smoke on school grounds, smokers congregate in front of the fence along the street before and after school in full view of the community.

The parking lots in front of the school are reserved for faculty and visitors; students park at the rear. As a policeman guards the student parking lot during the school day, many students prefer to park along the streets near the school where their cars are available during the day in case they want to skip out for awhile.

Almost 2,000 of the school's 2,700 students use the orange and black school buses; the constant arrivals and departures of these buses before and after school provide an important element of tension to the school day. The bus that doesn't come, the danger of students rushing to get seats, unpleasant relations between bus drivers and students, and supervision of students while buses are loading are elements of tension that bussing produces in the life of the school.

THROUGH THE GATES

One must enter the school by the main entrance because all other doors are locked. This policy of locking the other doors started shortly after the present principal came. After describing a situation in a school where two students had had intercourse in an empty, unlocked classroom, he informed the staff that we were all to keep our classroom doors locked at all times when we were not in our rooms, and that we were responsible for what went on in our classroom if we left the door unlocked. All the classroom locks were changed, and rigid control of new master keys made classrooms more impregnable.

The next step was locking the school. With the classrooms locked, the students roamed the halls. Locking the building exits proved ineffective because, even when locked, the doors open from the inside. The final step was chaining the doors. The janitors keep all the doors to the school, except the main entrance, locked at all times. At four o'clock they also chain the doors so that one not only can't get in but can't get out. They lock the main entrance at four but do not chain it until later. One student working on the yearbook got in on a Saturday morning by special arrangement without the janitor's knowledge. The janitor chained the entrance, and she did not manage to get out until evening.

If a teacher stays after four o'clock, he has to go all the way to the main entrance to get out. If he wants to return evenings or weekends, he must make special arrangements to get into the school. Faculty sponsors of activities struggle constantly to make the school available to the students to carry on their activities. The county recreation workers gained the use of the school on Saturday mornings only after a bitter contest with the school authorities. Adult education classes at the school make it possible to get in the school weekday evenings in spite of all these controls.

Even this policy of locking doors does not keep undesirable people out. Frequent raids of the bank, cafeteria, and office do much damage to the property, although the marauders find nothing of value. Money and other valuables are locked into the vault every night, and the amateur thieves lack the skill it takes to get in there.

These locked doors alienate pupils, teachers, and others. Teachers cannot keep files and bulletin boards in good shape without extra time to work on them. Students enthusiastic over some phase of extracurricular activity lose interest and drop out if frequently rebuffed. Parents feel strange, as though they did not belong in the school, when the doors won't open to them. Alumni are especially sensitive to the inhospitality the locked doors connote, and even the alumni association party at Christmastime is now held outside the school. Regulations require alumni wishing to visit teachers to obtain a visitor's pass, and this may be refused. The principal believes that such visits are a nuisance to the teachers even though some teachers feel a need for contact with alumni, not only for the satisfaction the students bring when they care enough to come back, but also for the information they report. What did the alumni learn in their classes that was useful to them after they left the school? What was missing in their training? Answers to these questions are important guides in curriculum development. However justified, the locked doors are a problem to participating personnel.

Entering the entrance hall by the door at the center of the building, one finds the school seal, mounted on the floor and surrounded by a velvet railing, dominating the hall. This was a gift of a recent senior class. Behind this often stands a papier-mâché replica of Terry Tiger, the school mascot. Terry towers about 8 feet and is striped red and white, the school colors. Glass-encased bulletin boards on each side of this entrance publicize a variety of school functions.

A ceiling drop at the rear of this entrance has been put to several uses. When the present principal took office, he had his favorite quotation about education painted there: "Wisdom is the principal thing, therefore get wisdom; and with all thy getting get understanding." One of our former art teachers, a modern art enthusiast, covered this with a mural depicting the history of man. The suggestion of embryonic development in the painting prompted some teachers to criticize it as inappropriate, and the mural subsequently disappeared beneath a soft, cream-colored coat of paint.

ALONG THE PATHS

The main hallway of the school is so long that if a person stands at one end, he cannot see to the other. Built-in lockers line its terrazzo floors, and the ceiling lights are recessed. Large clocks, set at right angles to the wall and spaced at regular intervals, provide instant time wherever a student may be. Of course, the time is not always correct, but the hardware is there, nevertheless.

Bulletin boards also grace the main-floor hallways. The bank and the library both have glassed-in recessed bulletin boards, which usually contain clever and artistic presentations of appropriate subjects. By the office door is a school calendar neatly done with white plastic letters on a blue felt background. Also the student council and the guidance departments have bulletin boards in the main hall. The guidance one is typically a clutter of information about jobs and colleges. The student-council bulletin board seldom excites comment and is often left up too long.

The junior and senior classes have large bulletin boards facing each other at the end of the wing leading to the cafeteria, and the sophomores have one at the far end of the same hall. The three classes compete with one another in offering clever, attractive presentations of class activities or attitudes. At times these boards become marked, are torn up, or have materials stolen from them.

Wherever the halls touch outside walls, they are lined with windows. The windows are seldom clean, sometimes broken.

Before and after school and between classes milling, jabbering students jam these halls. The teacher who walks through them, however, when the school is empty can capture the excitement and romance of education as at no other time. These pathways are full of memories of students long gone and the challenge of those to come, and the quietness can touch the teacher in somewhat the same manner that a parent responds to the sight of his sleeping child.

THE CONTROL CENTER

The main office is flanked by the principal's office on the right and the office of one of the vice-principals on the left. A long row of chairs faces the counter, and here the students wait for discipline. Four secretaries and numerous student helpers behind the counter are courteous and even kind to students. A steady flow of traffic goes through the office, where business is conducted to the accompaniment of the buzzing and bell ringing of the switchboard. A large letter box contains cubbyholes labeled with each teacher's name alphabetically arranged.

The principal's office has a curtain at right angles to the door. This provides some degree of privacy but permits the "open door" policy of the principal. Unless a major conference is in session, the door is open, and anyone can enter without being announced.

His office itself is carpeted and furnished with a sofa, two upholstered chairs, a mahogany desk, and several comfortable straight chairs. A private bath opens off the room. Between the principal's office and the hall is the public address room, which is small but mighty. A door from the principal's office to the PA room gives the principal control over this nerve center of the school.

Although the school is too large for an assembly of full personnel, the PA, reaching into every nook and cranny of the school, serves as the one possible unifying factor. A small speaker in each classroom, which is loud enough to be heard in the halls, carries the sound from the PA room to every part of the building. Once some students jammed the system so badly it never recovered. A new system, after a painful period of adjustment, works well.

The PA is used for opening exercises, which are planned and executed by the Broadcasting Club of the school under the supervision of the speech teacher. Occasionally a talented student gets a turn at conducting them and may sound good, but most of the time the PA program is stilted and dull. The programs begin with a moment of "inspiration" in the form of a quotation of some kind, followed by the Pledge of Allegiance to the flag of the United States. This gesture seems even hollower with the omission of the Lord's Prayer, which used to follow it. The announcements which follow are generally brief, because most of the announcements are read in the classroom from dittoed sheets. Sometimes the principal uses the opening exercises to commend the success of a school activity, or someone else briefly publicizes a special event. Once a week, the "Memories Girls" poke fun at a senior by digging up embarrassing anecdotes from his childhood, and on Friday each week a male student gives a brief roundup of school sports news.

On the PA the process of giving directions may become a

comedy of errors. The simple matter of addressing PTA notices can assume surprisingly complex proportions. The administrator, by a process of mind changing, makes decisions as he goes along regarding procedure and goes into so much detail it becomes confusing. Which side is up suddenly may become a highly controversial issue, and while the classes stir in mass confusion, the administrator continues on his way, unaware of the havoc spread throughout the school.

The PA is also interruptive. According to some reports, our school is better than most in this respect. Emergency announcements come on the PA at 1:30 before fifth-period classes start. However, announcements so important they can't wait, like cars in the way and a need for a janitor, may intrude at any time. If a teacher is involved in an important discussion, this can be unnerving. Once, concluding a demonstration of a personality analysis, I was reading a poem to a hushed class. I moved eloquently into the climactic lines from Edwin Markham's *Lincoln, the Man of the People:*

> *And when he fell in whirlwind, he went down*
> *As when a lordly cedar, green with boughs,*
> *Goes down with a great shout upon the hills,*
> *And leaves a lonesome place against the sky.*

The PA click sounded with a bomblike effect at the end of the first two lines. The last two lines were never read, and the point of the lesson was dulled, perhaps forever. It's just as bad when a student has something he is trying to say, gets interrupted by the PA, and then can't remember what had once been so important. Sometimes classes are so dull that even a PA interruption can be almost welcome, but most of the time teachers and students alike resent it.

The bank is at the left of the main entrance and across from the main office. It has two barred windows with small counters in front for students' use. Inside are a desk for the teacher-supervisor and worktables for students who operate the bank. The bank collects all monies except special classroom fees, sells all tickets, and offers savings account services to the students.

THE LIBRARY

On the right of the main entrance is the library. This is a beautiful high-ceilinged room of books and highly polished walnut tables and chairs. Students' paintings hang above the bookshelves, and fresh flowers often decorate the librarian's desk and the check-out counter. A soundproof partition, glass from waist height to ceiling, separates the reading room from the reference room, which is often used for instructional purposes.

Here the windows are as tall as the vaulted ceilings and are covered with white venetian blinds. Waist-high shelves, filled with a variety of encyclopedias and other reference materials, line the room. A front desk serves the student librarian who locates the periodical materials in the stacks in the room behind. The rest of the room is filled with rows of long tables, and all chairs face the front. At the rear of this room are two small rooms, one for the assistant librarian and one for the faculty. The faculty room contains a professional library, a photocopy machine, and a coffee urn.

Circulating books are in the other section of the library. Shelves line the room, and a series of stacks stand at the rear. Small tables have chairs which face each other, and some magazine racks are near an arrangement of leather chairs and sofa. A small table by the exit door bears the sign, "Please show your books before leaving." The staff decided on the necessity of the book check after three sets of encyclopedias were broken because of disappearing books. A cavelike visual-aid room, which is jammed with equipment, opens off this room.

The library is the heart of the school, and the persons who work there help to make it so. People are important here, and everyone is always welcome. The place is usually filled to capacity so that often the room becomes stuffy. Teachers arrange with the librarian to bring entire classes to the library, and both rooms are frequently scheduled weeks ahead. The library not only must turn students away because of overcrowding, but must always deal with the problem of stacking the constant inflow of new books.

GUIDANCE

Across from the library is the guidance department, a long narrow windowless room with office space built-in at one end and four counselor's rooms opening off it along one side. Along the wall opposite the doors are some tables and chairs where students can work while waiting their turns. Student paintings and a large bulletin board decorate the wall. Two racks of guidance materials provide vocational information and college catalogs.

On the wall opposite the entrance is a sign, "Sign up here for conferences." A pad, pencil, and drop box provide the facilities for doing so. Six guidance counselors and one clerk serve 2,600 students. The fact that guidance staff are responsible for individual student records reduces most counseling activity to record keeping. Counselors help students decide their school program, and a college counselor helps the seniors arrange college admission. Counselors also sometimes advise students with problems in student-faculty relationships. Other than this, little individual personal counseling is possible. The overburdened counselors are seldom available in a crisis. They are strangers to the students and are often able to do no more than listen to their problems, if that much.

A case history might be illustrative.

Jane came in after school one day to see me about an assignment. She remained until five o'clock, describing in almost anguished tones the problem of her close friendship with her girl friend Fran. She and Fran had a great need to see each other, but they had been forbidden to do so by both their families. The next morning, just as my first-period class was getting under way, I saw Jane and another girl standing in the hall outside my door. Jane looked distressed.

"This is Fran," she declared as I went out to investigate. "She ran away from home last night, and I brought her to school with me today. The office won't give her a visitor's pass, and we don't know what to do. I think I should leave with her."

"I'm certain there is a better solution," I said. "Let's go up and talk to the guidance counselor."

Knowing they would leave school if I didn't go with them, I put my class to work and went to the guidance office with them. All the counselors were out in the English classes inviting the students to come to guidance when they had a problem. We went to the office where I, with pressure, persuaded the principal to allow Fran to remain in the library until we could contact a counselor. Jane agreed to return to class until a conference with the counselor would be arranged.

I explained the situation to the counselor as soon as I could reach her, and she agreed we should keep the girls in school. But by then Jane, who is naturally shy, had become even more upset and refused to talk to the counselor. Fran stayed in my class the rest of the day. During a talk after school, Fran decided to return to her home, and for the moment, the crisis was over.

11

Many faculty members consider counseling a status job in the school, not only because of the higher salary scale, but also because of the freedom from classroom responsibilities. In practice, however, counseling is the most frustrating of positions because so much that needs to be done is beyond the capacity of the counselor.

OTHER SPECIALIZED AREAS

The special classrooms most impressed our visitor from abroad. Science rooms are laboratories. Business rooms have office equipment. The home economics department has a completely equipped kitchen, sewing room, apartment, and laundry. The shop department includes a wood shop, a metal shop, a print shop, and a drafting room. Two soundproof rooms contain tiered floors for the band and the chorus. The language department has a laboratory complete with the newest electronic equipment. The reading improvement room is also a laboratory. The three art rooms have high tables, stools, and large, flat drawers for storing drawings as well as built-in cupboards for storing supplies. Two gymnasiums offer separate facilities for boys and girls.

Next to the guidance office is the health room, consisting of three sections—a waiting room, the nurse's office, and a 2-bed infirmary. The health room is a pleasant and friendly place despite the constant battle against hypochondria.

Beyond the health room, at the end of the hall, is the school store. The store is the responsibility of students in the salesmanship classes. Here students can buy school supplies, paperback books assigned in class, and such school promotion articles as seals and emblems for notebooks, school jackets, and little tigers. The store is open before and after school, and it usually attracts a long line of student customers.

The cafeteria, at the far end of the first wing, is a vast place. An extension to the end of the entire wing doubled the original size of the cafeteria. It looks wider than a football field and is longer than it is wide. Its low acoustical-tile ceiling is divided by a ceiling drop, and a series of support posts mark off the original from the extension. The familiar cinder-block walls are painted a pastel shade.

Attractive table-chair combinations seat ten to a table, fold up easily, and can be rolled away almost effortlessly. A row of windows on the far side has venetian blinds artistically draped with dark blue wool left over from a prom in the distant past. Across the front of the room is a long low window for receiving trays, three full-lunch serving lines, and a serving line for sandwiches, milk, ice cream, and doughnuts.

The faculty has a crowded but private lunch room, achieved through a label "Committee Room" on the architectural plans. The cafeteria is supervised by teachers who carry a lighter teaching load to compensate for this responsibility.

The food in the cafeteria is excellent, although the students grumble about it quite a bit. The generous servings are sometimes too much for an ordinary adult, but some of the still-growing boys eat two lunches every day. Many days, more than one menu is available, and tempting extra desserts are always on sale. The lunches are partially supported by the government lunch program and are only thirty-five cents for the students. Ice cream and pie are sold at the usual restaurant prices, but milk is only a penny a carton.

The board of education went overboard on the auditorium. Seating accommodations with luxurious upholstery are provided for 1,400 people; it is carpeted and velvet-curtained. An artistically designed vaulted ceiling with narrowing walls approaching the stage provides a somewhat dramatic atmosphere. A variation of wall color adds excitement to the cinder-block interior. Although the lighting and acoustics are good, the balcony is disappointing because not much can be seen from the seats in the rear section. Little daytime use is made of the auditorium, even though the band practices on the stage every day that the auditorium is free. Perhaps its limited use is related to the fact that only half the student body can be seated at one time, and therefore the scheduling of assembly programs becomes complicated.

This picture of the school is incomplete, from the students' point of view, without a description of the bathrooms. From a physical standpoint, they are like most public bathrooms. The entrance is arranged so that no view of the room is possible when the door is open. For the girls, a row of toilets opposes a row of round sinks, and a large mirror on the wall tops a tall trash can. A comfortable space for hiding between the last toilet and the window is enhanced by a ledge about a foot high from the floor below frosted windows.

This seat was designed, probably, to accommodate the heating system.

For students the bathroom is a retreat. Some teachers permit the bored student to seek out this refuge and pay little attention to how long he stays. This is a place to get a couple of drags on the forbidden cigarette between classes or during the lunch hour. Some who bring their lunches even prefer to eat in the bathroom in order to smoke afterward. This is the only place in school where a student can go to cry. It is also a place to go when a student feels sick, when his clothes need repairing, or just when he needs to see how he looks.

Most bathrooms are dirty. Obscene writing and lipstick appear on the walls, and paper towels are strewed on the floors. The sinks are sometimes clogged because of junk left in them, and cigarette butts often lie on the floor where someone didn't have time or didn't bother to flush them down the toilet. In the boys' rooms, fires occasionally start in trash cans. If a bathroom gets beyond control, the administrators simply lock the door, forcing the students to keep looking until they find an open one.

This, then, is the school, providing generously for the physical needs of our educational system. My guest from Indochina had reason to be impressed. Since this school resembles a cage to some, we must look for other factors to understand the reasons why.

CHAPTER TWO

They Pace

OUTSIDE THE CLASSROOM WALLS

"As I walk from one class to the next I can hear many conversations . . . people making plans to meet after school at someone's car, discussing last period's exam, whether they should cut next period, or should they buy a ticket to the next football game . . . ," writes Jay Hardin, a senior.

Caged in the zoo, the lion paces to relieve his tension. Outside the classroom students also pace, and here they find more than mere release. They find each other. Just as in a modern zoo the observer may get the impression of freedom for the animals as he looks across a chasm that confines them, so one may feel the thrust of vitality of youth as they move about the cage.

The students are usually well dressed and well groomed because the self-consciousness of adolescence focuses on physical appearance first. Boys are as conscious and careful of their appearance as girls. Styles at the present time are highly decorous, although a fad for tight-fitting off-white jeans seems to be coming in for the boys. And, of course, the skirts are tight and short for the girls who now have no modest sitting position.

Some girls spend a week's salary earned on their part-time jobs for a glamorous outfit and then wear it only once, because one of the challenges of being well dressed is to be able to go several months without wearing the same thing twice. The girl selected as the best-dressed girl of the senior class last year has four sisters all about her size. She probably did not repeat an outfit once during the year.

Sophomores, more than upper classmen, tend to go to extremes on their styles: weird hairdos, very short skirts, and heavy makeup for the girls; tight pants and needle-pointed shoes for the boys. During the high school years, students show definite growth in ability to make the most of their appearance. Rarely is even a sophomore slovenly, dirty, or uncombed, however.

A significant phenomenon in the school is the hall grouping which occurs before school starts in the morning. Students start arriving by bus as early as 8:00, and the late bell does not ring until 8:55. When a student arrives at school, he usually goes to his spot in the hall. Here he meets with his own particular group of friends and passes the time of day until the last possible minute he can make it to homeroom without penalty.

Walking the halls before school is a revealing experience. Most of the sophomores have homerooms in the basement, and their rendezvous spots are here. Horseplay among the boys, screaming and running back and forth among the girls, and romantic activity between the sexes are common. Fighting is a serious offense, but it occurs sometimes anyway. A gathering crowd is a sign of trouble. An element of danger exists in breaking up a fight because young tempers flash hot, and a woman teacher will sometimes seek a man in such a situation. The pitch of excitement in the halls varies greatly with the time of year. Tension grows when grading periods are ending or holidays starting. In the spring, both fighting and romance increase perceptibly.

Lovemaking in the halls shocks some. The principal has decreed that holding hands is acceptable, but anything beyond that unseemly for high school halls. Couples stand close, face to face, sometimes with their arms around each other. Kissing occurs also in varying degrees from light pecks to full motion-picture styles. Such behavior goes unchallenged most of the time primarily because it embarrasses teachers to interfere. Many youngsters actively resent reprimands for such behavior from teachers. Some other students, however, may criticize this behavior, feeling it does little credit to the school. One of my classes once hypothesized that lovemaking in the halls was more frequently practiced by sophomores than by seniors and attempted to make a survey. The plan was to approach lovers with the question, "Are you sophomores?" each time they were observed and make a record of the responses. Although no conclusions were reached, the students enjoyed the investigation.

Seniors occupy the main-floor halls. Circles of conversation groups occur up and down these halls. The football circle has the place of honor at the intersection of the B wing and main hall. Nearby the cheerleaders have a spot, and the status level of the students decreases with its distance from the center. Although the football circle gets a little rowdy at times, for the most part the seniors are far more sophisticated and dignified in their hall behavior than the sophomores down below. Although much teasing and shouting occurs, their behavior seldom takes the form of excessive physical activity. The junior homerooms are on the second floor, and the hall behavior of juniors marks the transition from the rowdy sophomores to the dignified seniors.

Movement in the halls between classes is rapid and easy save for friends who stop to chat in the middle of the traffic flow and cause jams. Some of the central halls become seriously clogged at times because of this, but generally the students are patient, and pushing seldom gets rough.

THE KEEPERS BREAK THE PACE

Teachers are alien objects in the halls, in a sense, because they carry with them a certain objectionable supervisory responsibility. Inside the classroom, teachers can tender the task of molding the students into necessary patterns of conformity with individual care and treatment, but in the halls this cannot be done to any great extent. Here the teacher is like a cop on the beat, only the club that gives the cop security is missing. Teachers have to depend on sheer force of personality to maintain discipline in any part of the school areas where they do not know the identity of the students. An identified student can be punished, but a student can easily give a false name if the teacher doesn't know him, and teachers always run the risk of being ridiculed when they discipline in the halls.

A teacher develops "that look"—an expression done primarily with the eyes that says, "I am right and you are wrong! Get out of my hair!" This look is mean, condemnatory, and almost violent. Using it is not pleasant and not necessary in a classroom, but it works in the halls. Two boys wrestling in the hall quail and withdraw when they see it. Lovers flush and pull apart. Some teachers go through the halls as though they were wearing blinders. If they see no evil and hear no evil, they avoid unpleasant relations, but they thus tacitly encourage lawbreaking. Students don't like "the look," but they are confused by the inconsistency of adults who ignore their wrongdoing.

Students are sensitive about having teachers speak to them in the halls. In such a large school, the only identity most students achieve is in the classroom. If the teacher who knows him and responds to him there doesn't recognize him in the hall, the student feels that the identity he has in the classroom is just a name on a seating chart. Most teachers are aware of this and try to be alert to students who are expecting it. This requires full concentration, however, and often a teacher fails to recognize a passing student.

Sometimes teachers create resentment. They have privileges in school that are denied students, such as smoking and breaking in the lunch line. Students who have been suspended for smoking on school property sneer when they see smoke billowing out of the faculty room. Before the cafeteria was enlarged, the faculty used to break in the lunch line, and many hungry students chafed beneath the surface. Now the faculty has a special line which works much better. Wherever faculty members break rules that students are expected to accept, resentment flows quite freely.

The picture is not entirely grim, however. Sometimes, when I was at an ebb tide in my personal life and needed a lift, I was guilty of making an unnecessary trip through the halls. I chose a well-traveled route where discipline problems were not likely to occur and walked fast, calling by name each student that I recognized. By the time I returned to my room, I felt good again, because each time a student responded to my greeting, I felt afresh the vigor of youth. The students I taught were reaching so eagerly for life that their response to such friendliness could make me feel alive and vital.

Because of the acoustical properties of the cafeteria, the noise level of the lunchroom is quite tolerable. The lunch lines are long, but they move swiftly, and lunch-line hopping is fairly uncommon. Here the students are free to choose the friends with whom they eat, and these lunch groups become very important to them.

This bit of free choice was threatened one year in the opening days of school.

Because students the year before had done a shoddy job cleaning up their tables after eating, the principal ordered the faculty to assign lunch tables to their fourth-period class so that responsibility could be traced. The faculty, busy with a multitude of opening-of-school details, was lax about turning in the necessary lists. Of course, the students were furious with the prospect. The new vice-principal who was in charge of the cafeteria learned of this and, deciding to try giving the students another chance, postponed the table-assignment plan.

Most students remain at the tables with their friends until the bell releases them. An occasional birthday cake brightens the picture, and at some seasons, organized shouting can be heard all the way back in the faculty room. In spite of faculty supervision and student council efforts, students leave dirty lunch tables and floors, creating a serious problem for the next group.

To many students, the cafeteria is one of the most important places in the school. For some, eating is the high point of the school day. For others, the chance to socialize is more important. Students must remain in the lunchroom until five minutes before the bell. Occasionally a student prefers to skip lunch rather than be so confined, especially a loner who has found no friendship group at the lunch table.

Supervising assemblies is difficult. Auditorium manners leave much to be desired partly because the students have had few opportunities to learn them. Until the auditorium was completed, the school had no assemblies. When assemblies convened in the auditorium, good programs went well, but if the interest lagged, general conversation took over. Actual shouting and whistling broke out in one senior class meeting when an unpleasant issue arose, and that class had no further meetings.

Students waiting for buses are a challenge to a teacher supervising them, but also fun. (Faculty coverage is required because of insurance regulations, but much actual control is impractical.) Before the students started smoking beyond the fence line, a teacher asked at a faculty meeting, "What should we do if we see a student we don't know smoking when we are on bus duty?"

"Turn your head," was the answer.

Students rush to load the buses, crowding and pushing to be first in line, and the danger of the one in front being pushed into a moving bus is great. Students respond to faculty control if the bus driver holds the door until control is established, but some of the drivers are in a bigger hurry than the students. Generally, teachers just stand back and watch them scramble.

Most of the students behave well otherwise. They are glad to get out of school, and often stand and chat with their friends. Some patronize the ice cream wagon or cross the fence line for a smoke. Students often pleasantly converse with teachers on duty if they know them, and the time goes quickly.

WHEN THEY PLAY

Once a week during the various sports seasons, students who purchase tickets are excused for athletic events. Generally students feel they are buying their way out of school. For the indoor sports, the teachers guard the doors, since fire regulations prohibit chaining these doors during the day. The students are thus forced to remain for the game. For the outdoor sports, however, students must leave the building to get to the game, and droves of them leave the school grounds as well, crossing the hill to a shopping plaza. The behavior during athletic events is wild. Smoking, swearing, and serious fighting occur frequently. Cheering is a disheartening process in spite of the efforts of a hard-working group of cheerleaders. The stands are almost empty by 3:30 regardless of the state of the game.

In the past, students have attempted to extend their pacing with various kinds of informal activities about the school. One of these was Sadie Hawkins Day. This is the day when the students dressed up in hillbilly outfits in honor of Lil' Abner and Daisy Mae. Boys made the girls carry their books and, in return, agreed to go with them to the Sadie Hawkins dance that night where Marryin' Sam, the principal, "married" one of the couples. The outfits were ingenious, and practically all the students participated. It was a day of great excitement and self-consciousness and fun. When first gathered in the classroom, the students looked around at the most outstanding outfits, laughed over them, and then settled down to normal classroom behavior when the bell rang. As soon as the class was over, they were off again on the same high pitch of excitement with which they entered. Then we had an announcement. We would have no more Sadie Hawkins Days because the principals of the county had ruled against them. Apparently in some of the schools students had indulged in an overdose of rowdyism.

Before the board of education outlawed smoking areas on the school grounds as a result of the evidence published by the U.S. Public Health Service on the relationship between smoking and lung cancer, the school had a smoking area known to the students as the "smokin' hole." This was a section of blacktop behind the multipurpose room in the B wing. Much living took place here: It was a rendezvous for fights; penny pitching spiraled to pitching fifty-cent pieces; hearts soared and broke; and debates on the existence of God or the best sports car model occurred. When the new addition was completed, the smoking area moved to a concrete section under the cafeteria. Students, interested in fixing this up to give it an air of respectability, discussed plans for providing benches, attractive trash cans, and music. About that time the board of education made its ruling and banned the smoking areas. Much to the surprise of all the adult personnel in the school, the students accepted this new ruling with a minimum of rebellion. Patrolled bathrooms revealed little smoking. Gradually the problem has developed in subsequent years to the point that the ruling is objectionable to students and faculty alike, but behavior at football games, where no control over smoking is even attempted, indicates that fewer students smoke now than did when smoking areas existed on the school grounds.

One year a Breakfast Club sprang up in the cafeteria. The cafeteria staff served juice, doughnuts, and milk to students who wanted them in the morning before school. A couple of sophomore boys, one of whom walked only with crutches and braces on his paralyzed legs, started banging on an old piano down there one morning. The students liked the atmosphere, and the boys began to play regularly. Before long, the cafeteria became a social center mornings before school. Some students undertook responsibility for maintaining the Breakfast Club. They borrowed a record player from the library to supplement the piano playing with canned music when it was needed, and supervised the clearing of the tables. By then the cafeteria was jammed with students, and keeping the tables clean had become a problem.

The Breakfast Club died as quickly as it was born. The cafeteria had to be used for homeroom space, and breakfast could no longer be served. One big useless effort was made to move the breakfast serving to the multipurpose room and develop that space into a lounge area, which failed because the wrestling group used that room for wrestling practice. The wrestlers locked the room when not using it because they stored their very expensive wrestling mats there. In a vandalism spree, someone broke in and knifed one of those mats to shreds some years later.

Another year the seniors developed a senior lounge. The band had moved to the auditorium, which left the band room free most of the time. The seniors got a coke machine and a candy machine for this room, and the president of the senior class had a key so he could open it mornings for senior use. They put pompons, the fluffy balls that pompon girls use at football games, around the shelves and had plans for adding drapes and card tables to improve the atmosphere. Vandalism became a serious problem in the school that year, and someone broke into the room and jammed the machines, seriously damaging them. The next day the machines were carted down the hall and out of the building, and the senior lounge no longer operated. The students who had promoted the lounge were so discouraged over the criticism constantly rendered them that it was a relief to turn away from it.

The parking lot was once an important social center also. Although it was off bounds during the day according to regulations, it nevertheless provided facilities for sexual gratification, smoking, eating lunch, drinking, and sometimes just a place to get away. After arranging for a private policeman for protection of the parking lot, the principal announced to the faculty, "This is the best thing that has happened to our school since I have been here." The student parking lot is now at the rear of the building where the policeman carefully guards cars and activity during the school hours. Fewer cars are there, and no students at all during the day.

A CLOSER FOCUS

Thus the chasm is there, and the students are confined in their pacing. Even confined pacing has value, however, as illustrated by a look at the day of an individual student. As Tom moves about the school from class to class, his relationships with his fellow students embroider his school life, giving it meaning and body.

Tom is a sophomore. He is a year behind in school because of a slow maturation pattern, but he is a good student, maintaining a B average with very little effort. He is conscientious and self-directed about homework, but his interests center on his dance band, his friends, and his guppies.

He walks to school, leaving home at 8:25 and making stops to pick up Chuck and Carl. These three boys have known each other since the age of two and are fondly referred to by their parents as the three musketeers. Carl is a junior and Chuck a sophomore who is a year younger than the other two. On the way to school, Tom talks to Chuck about amplifying their instruments and to Carl about the war in Vietnam. They all talk about the Catholic grade school youngsters they have to wade through to get to school. They arrive at school just in time to make it to homeroom and split up for the day.

Tom goes to homeroom in the A wing. If he has time, he goes to his locker first. He uses his orchestra locker, which is nearby and large enough to accommodate his instruments and belongings and those of his friend in orchestra, Bert. He, along with the rest of the homeroom students, slides into the room after the warning bell.

The dismissal bell releases Tom to go to his locker, get his books for his morning classes, and then go up the stairs to the top floor for English. He usually sees Chuck on the way up, but they don't have time for more than a greeting. He does find time to stop at the water fountain, though. He stops at every water fountain he sees all day long.

When he leaves English class, he walks down to biology with Joe Greene, who shares both classes with him. They stop in the bathroom on the way down, where he usually sees Carl long enough to exchange a few sentences.

He has to rush to get to orchestra because he is always the last to get out of biology class, and he has to go back to the auditorium stage in the new wing. In this class the teacher, Mr. Aldrich, leaves for another school when the orchestra is excused to put their instruments away, and the students are on their honor to stay until they are supposed to leave. Since this is the end of the third period, seniors have the privilege of leaving two minutes early to be first in the lunch line.

Tom's German class has a split lunch period. This means that he goes one half hour to class, then to lunch, and back for the second half of class. He changes his books from those for morning classes to those for afternoon classes before he leaves orchestra and walks part way with Richard. He stops at a bathroom and drinking fountain again on the way. He sees many students he knows from grade school and junior high school as he goes through the halls because high school has become a meeting place for the divergent paths he has trod, but he doesn't have time to say more than "Hi."

Tom charges down the hall when the lunch bell rings to get an early place in line. He buys a full lunch, two extra cartons of milk, and pie. He has two lunch groups. If something is going on in German class that he wants to discuss, he sits with his grade school chum, where a group from his German class also sits. Generally, however, he sits with some of his friends from junior high, and they joke around a lot. There everyday Ted tries to sell the extra cookies in his lunch. Nobody ever buys them, and he crumbles them to pieces. Tom returns his tray when he has finished eating and gets one, two, or sometimes even three ice creams to finish off his lunch. He goes back to his lunch table, sometimes changing to the group he did not eat with, and remains until the release bell rings. The boys put on an act of not cleaning up their lunch table, but always leave it in good shape.

After the second half of German class, Tom goes down to the basement level toward C wing for his geometry class. Sixth period livens up with physical education. Here he has many friends from previous school experiences, and he doesn't even mind the exercises with which they start the period.

At 3:30, he goes back to his locker in A wing if necessary, but most of his homework is in German and math, and he has those books with him. When he wears a jacket, he must go back to his locker, of course, but either way he meets Carl and Chuck at the phone booth in front of the main entrance to the school, and they walk home together. On the homeward trek, they are frequently joined by other friends who live in the neighborhood. None of them are likely to stay for club meetings.

This sample of a typical day in the life of the school shows to a small degree how a student's relations with his friends in school enrich his school life. The bulk of a student's time, however, is spent within the classroom. We must turn to see what happens there if we are to understand the cage and its influence.

CHAPTER THREE

They Crouch

CLASSROOM CLIMATES

*"When I sit in a classroom, I feel trapped. I loathe
the desks and chairs and pupils and discipline.
Education is vital, but the fact that an unwilling minor
must sit for six hours in six different classes because
he or she needs a high school diploma to make it
in the world is no insurance that knowledge is
being acquired,"* writes Jane Ransom, a senior.

Confined to the classroom, the students crouch, victims of the circumstances that bind them there. In these cages within the larger cage, the major part of the taming process occurs.

Teaching is an art, and the classroom is the canvas on which the painting grows. The rooms all start out much the same. Large windows, covered with cream-colored cloth blinds that never quite work, line the far side of the room. Below the windows three tiers of bookshelves stand empty unless cluttered with dusty papers or broken books. A blackboard, now a modern green, fronts the room, and soft green cork bulletin boards, so large they take all the space from desk level almost to the ceiling, cover the other walls. Furniture varies somewhat, but all rooms include a desk, chair, and filing cabinet for the teacher and movable desk chairs for the students. A pencil sharpener, wastebasket, and American flag are also standard equipment. As they gain status in the school, teachers acquire extra furniture, which may include a table, several straight chairs, a storage cabinet, or an extra filing cabinet.

Room keeping is a difficult chore of teaching. Chalk dust, wastepaper from students' desks, settling dust from people passing through, or dirt tracked in from undrained sidewalks provide a constant challenge to a teacher whose attention is more likely focused on lesson plans, student demands, or administrative details.

This challenge becomes clear, perhaps, with an illustration of its importance in an incident which occurred when our new principal took office:

The former principal, loved by students, parents, and most of the faculty, had died of cancer at the height of his career. The aura of hero worship surrounding him resulted partly from the fact that he never criticized. He believed the school and everyone in it was perfect and got ulcers trying to sustain this belief.

Early in the fall the new principal summoned a number of teachers to his office and severely reprimanded them because of the badly marked student desks in their rooms. He informed them that teachers were responsible for the care of school property in their classrooms, that the condition of the desks reflected poor teaching, and that he expected them to mend their ways.

Apparently, the principal had walked into a trap. He had instructed the head custodian to inspect the desks and give him a list of teachers whose desks were in the worst condition. The head custodian, resenting the new intruder, had picked teachers whose reprimand would most affront the teachers themselves as well as other members of the faculty rather than those with badly marked desks. This action created much disturbance not only because most of the faculty felt that the condition of students' desks was not a sensible measure of competence, but also because some of the best teachers were so humiliated.

Although the rooms start out basically alike, they soon reflect the personality of the teacher and take on an individuality of their own. In the rare moments teachers have in their classrooms during pre-school faculty sessions, they make decisions which set the classroom scene.

One of these is the way they arrange the furniture. Most classrooms have rows of chairs that might as well be anchored to the floor. This arrangement gives a formal effect to the classroom. Other teachers experiment with circle arrangements in which the students face each other. Such a classroom immediately becomes less teacher-centered. Other subtle differences also have their effect— for example, whether the desks face the board, the windows, or the door.

Teachers also assemble materials for classroom use. Some carefully store these in shelves and cabinets, and others deliberately strew them about the room, creating diversion, confusion, and sometimes even interest. As a "floater," a teacher who has no classroom of his own but uses a different room each hour while other teachers have their planning period, I stacked such materials on a book cart and pushed them from room to room. I not only needed them for classroom use, but also gained poise from the feeling of having such materials around.

Teachers decorate the room. Use of the generous bulletin-board space contributes much to the effect of a classroom. Some teachers ignore it; a fresh-starter puts up an ambitious display in the pre-school days and leaves it there for the entire year; a clutterbug relays all the materials that come across his desk to the bulletin board; a few cajole students into credible displays; some put student papers on display. Whatever use develops influences the effect of the classroom.

Growing things lace some rooms. Some rooms are neat, others

out of true in a careless kind of way, and still others cold and empty in spite of people and furniture. So, even though they start alike, each classroom develops a different kind of atmosphere.

Our supervisor made an interesting effort to train teachers by influencing their room-keeping techniques:

> She opposed the use of podiums, feeling they encouraged a teacher to lecture too much, and required all the teachers under her supervision who used podiums to state the reasons why in a letter to her. She was quite disgruntled at the replies she received. I tried to be funny in mine, claiming that by leaning on the unstable music rack on which I kept my notes I could relieve my aching feet, but what we all were saying in one way or another was you can't change a teacher's art by forcing him to abandon his natural materials.

THE TAMERS

The 130 teachers who staff our school provide the electricity that not only powers the educational system but also controls the climate of the cages which they direct. Although teachers vary in age, appearance, and temperament, they have some common characteristics. Occupational hazards, risks inherent in the nature of a task, account for part of these.

One occupational hazard of teaching is tired feet. The floors in a school are hard on feet, especially the terrazzo floors in the halls. Teachers, standing on their feet most of the day, get achy, tired feet. Rarely can a teacher sit when teaching. A certain command accrues from physical towering, and the mere sight of a teacher in action increases the level of attention of the students. Sometimes teachers sit on desks, and one teacher I knew used a tall stool. Most teachers, however, are on their feet all day, and those feet are tired. This makes teaching an exhausting process. This weariness is subtly depressing because it does not give the honest kind of fatigue that comes from muscle motion such as walking. Teachers are too tired by the time they get home to seek the kind of exercise they need to keep them in good physical tone.

Another occupational hazard is the imperative that a teacher has to be right. Of course, teachers can admit some ignorance and some error, but most of the time they must know their facts if they expect to command the respect of their students. Because of this, teachers develop techniques for avoiding careless errors. This has a subtle effect on a teacher's personality. Confidence accrued in this manner eventually creates an authoritarian thrust to the gentlest soul. Teachers have more difficulty than most other people seeing someone else's point of view, and many unduly condemn careless errors in others. Some become so concerned with perfecting details that they miss the picture the details are forming. Punctuation on a theme sometimes assumes more importance than what the student is trying to communicate. This need to be right also makes teachers so strongly individualistic that they are a difficult group to direct.

A third occupational hazard is the lack of adult associations. About the only people teachers see are students. Relationships with students can be and often are richly rewarding, but they do not compensate for the lack of adult association in a teacher's life. Eventually, if teachers' associations are essentially limited to teenagers, they lose rapport with adults. They tend to treat all people as they do students which makes the contacts they do achieve with adults unsatisfactory. People in each stage of life need the reinforcement of value systems and patterns of behavior typical of their own level. Teachers do have a planning period at school, and a few of the wise ones deliberately devote that hour to coffee chats with other faculty members. They must then, however, take their work home to do, for a teacher's work is never done. Few teachers maintain an adequate social life with other adults, and this lack often leaves them empty and dissatisfied with life in general.

The most serious occupational hazard of teachers is the problem of the cost of loving the students that they teach. Some teachers do not have this problem. If they are primarily concerned with subject matter instead of personalities, their most significant reward is the paycheck, although some satisfaction from a job well done occurs if this is their goal and they achieve it. Others learn early in their careers that they can't change the elements in the lives of the students that create the problems the students have and decide they should not allow themselves to care. These teachers usually wind up teaching neither subject matter nor students and lead highly frustrated lives. A third group cares. These teachers have their students in class 180 hours. About half that time goes into knowing them well enough to love them. Once the emotional bridge is established, learning and growing travel across it both ways. Then suddenly June arrives, and the students are gone forever. The teacher recovers in time to face a new group in the fall and repeat the process.

For these reasons, teachers are often weary, obdurate, frustrated, and worried, but they also have some good qualities in common. In high school, most teachers are intelligent and capable people. They must know more facts than the students they are teaching in order to maintain enough respect to keep the classroom going. Some teachers are keener than others, but they are all well above average. Many are quite talented in speaking, writing, and artistic skills.

Teachers dress well. The stereotype of the dowdy teacher is definitely out of date. If a slip shows one day, before the first hour ends a student is likely to whisper this shocking fact in the teacher's ear. Teachers' salaries are much improved, and none of them live at the poverty level. Many modern teachers are smartly styled, and they often develop individualized modes of fashion in which students take great interest. A conservative teacher wore elaborate jewelry which she collected from world travels; a short and heavy teacher had an interesting variety of attractive shoes; a man teacher always wore a flower in his lapel; an attractive, petite teacher refused to shorten her hemline in spite of rising fashions; I wore blue all the time.

The most endearing quality that teachers share is a gusto for doing. They are so involved in the educational process that they are "very" in everything they do. Some are very bigoted and work hard at teaching their bigotry; others are very critical and spend much effort at being critical; still others are very idealistic and dream dreams beyond compare. Whatever their approach, the element that is most consistent is an element of deep concern. Frustration almost seems to be a key to the door of life, because they are such vital people.

THE TEACHER SETS THE STAGE

More than anything else, a classroom reflects a teacher's personality. One important influence is the discipline level a teacher chooses to maintain. This level varies from one teacher to another, and one is not necessarily better than the other. Two of the best teachers in the school practiced two extremes:

One was a history teacher who demanded absolute order in her class. A student was humiliated if he so much as dropped a pencil there. No student in the school would willingly interrupt her class by entering it during the hour. Students claimed that even the PA trembled when it came on in her room. This teacher was much admired for her teaching skill by the students in her classes. One class presented her with a corsage one Mother's Day because, they said, "We are her children."

At the opposite extreme was a math teacher who was so skillful that some of her students got advanced college credit from her training. When she talked, everybody listened because they needed to hear what she was saying, but the rest of the time everyone did whatever he wished. At times this developed into mass confusion, but she never asked for order. This was the atmosphere in which she could function best.

Few teachers function well at either of these extremes. When things get out of order to the point that the confusion disturbs a teacher, then the teacher does something about it, and that is the discipline level that is maintained in that classroom.

Closely related to the factor of discipline level is the degree of formality exercised in a classroom. One teacher in the county addressed the students as Mister and Miss. This disturbed the supervisor because she was from Texas and accustomed to informality. However, dignity as the essence of a classroom works well for some teachers. They set this degree by the way they greet members of the class as they enter the room, the way they sit on a desk or stand during class, the procedures for taking roll, and the way they teach.

Teachers also influence a classroom by the degree to which they maintain rules. Some classes stream in from the halls after the bell rings; others are in their seats. Some teachers ignore chewing gum; others abhor it. Some classes are so busy keeping rules that they don't have much time for classwork; others seem to have no rules. I was sometimes rigid in observance of rules:

One of the rules often cited to us was that we were never to dismiss a class until the bell rang. We were cautioned against making sensible decisions on our own in this regard, because we might not understand the reasons why the bell might not ring.

One of my problems as a teacher was a tendency to concentrate deeply. If I got absorbed in something, I often lost almost all conscious contact with my environment. One morning we were waiting out an extended homeroom period. A grading period was ending, and I became interested in some papers (sometimes seeing how students do on a test is exciting). The class was quite out of order before I became aware of it, and when I looked up I discovered we had been waiting twenty minutes. My first-period class was stewing in the hall, and my homeroom students were boisterous and fuming.

Instead of dismissing my class as the other teachers had done, I sent a student to the office to tell them the bell hadn't rung. Soon an announcement came booming over the PA to the effect that these students were to be admitted late without penalty because they had not been dismissed. I felt foolish, but continued a strict adherence of rules in my classroom.

The underlying philosophy by which a teacher functions is the most important factor, however, in determining the nature of the classroom. A schoolroom is *not* democratic. As long as adults structure schools to convey from one generation to another the accumulated knowledge of a culture, a schoolroom will remain essentially autocratic.

Early in my teaching career, I was discussing teacher-pupil planning with my principal. "That's tricky," he declared. "I saw one teacher do a splendid job with it once, though. She spent the entire class period planning a unit with the group, and at the end of the hour they had developed the exact outline she had started with."

I never again discussed teacher-pupil planning with other adults in my school, but I did experiment with it and found a limited amount practical. The most successful teacher-pupil planning occurred, however, when I gave the students the content outline and let them develop the methods of approach. As long as the teacher has a definite curriculum to cover, the classroom is autocratic. Efforts in progressive education to change this approach have not been accepted in our system, and the present trend is toward greater structure rather than less.

A teacher with a democratic philosophy, however, can do much to influence the classroom atmosphere through the acceptance of each student as an individual. New teachers tend to be more democratic than more experienced ones. Because they have not been in the cage long enough to sense the drag of the system, they expect students to respond to what they have to offer, and accept students as they are without trying to change them. This often works well, and the first year of teaching may be the best in a teacher's career. The best of the experienced teachers maintain a high level of democratic practice in their relationships to individuals, but most teachers lose it in the process of becoming disciplinarians.

To many teachers the world is made up of good guys and bad guys, and their function as a teacher is to enjoy the good guys and reform the bad ones. This is not gloriously done by dealing with individuals, but massively done by teaching the class the way good guys should be taught and expecting the bad guys to join in the action. Thus conformity becomes the medium of reform. This is the antithesis of democracy, and even though widespread lip service to democracy occurs in our classrooms, little practice of it follows.

THE CROUCHING COUNTS

Although the teacher is the most important influence in determining the feel of a classroom, the students also set the tone. Each class has a personality as unique as every individual personality. A few years of substitute teaching impressed me with the richness of this variation. For every teacher, one class each year always seemed to be more of a chore than the others combined. Rather than describe a series of unusual classes, a more valid approach perhaps is to describe, as the basis of class personality analyses, the five classes I taught one year.

> My first-period class was "creative." One often finds creative individuals in classes, but this whole class was creative. Although they started out slowly with contributions to planning, during the last quarter of the year they developed their own classes in their own way with power and perception. They felt the class was theirs, and they allowed me to enjoy it. The ability level varied from low average to high with one quiet, brilliant student. Most of them had above-average ability, but not above-average grades. The president of the senior class and the captain of the drum majorettes were both in this class, but, interestingly enough, they were not the leaders of the class, although they were a vital part of it. The class contained poets, artists, a musician, and some big talkers. These students did clever bulletin boards, unusual skits, ridiculous experiments, and plunged into the philosophy of life unit with no holds barred. They were volatile, critical, and lazy, but most of all, they were creative.

> My second-period class was disunified. This group never became a unit. It was the class I could have done without, although they

gave no serious discipline problems. The students in it didn't care enough to bother. They went through the gestures of doing what the other classes did, and at times did them rather well but never with any enthusiasm. This class continued to be a collection of individuals to the very end of school.

My third class was eruptive. One girl in the class was uninhibited. In addition, she was beautiful, alive, idealistic, and emotional. She stirred the entire class to a level of participation that required constant admonitions on my part to keep even a semblance of order. The emotional tone of this class was so warm that at the beginning of the hour the students would come in the room and stay until the bell rang instead of putting their books down and going out in the hall to socialize until time for the bell, as is the custom.

My fourth-period class was polite. In response to what might have been a highly controversial question in other classes, one student here would raise his hand and answer the question; everyone would agree; and they would then turn to me for the next question. This sounds deadly, but it wasn't at all. The students were skillful, worked hard, and were interested in the subject. They did the activities with interest and originality, but they were always gentle and polite with their procedures. I tried to jar them loose one day and was quite critical, accusing them of complacency. The next day they all wore blue to class to see if I would notice. I didn't.

My fifth-period class was nice. They liked me, and they liked each other. Psychology classes were not grouped according to ability level, but about three-fourths of this class had below-average ability. Although the other fourth of the students were above average, they were well-adjusted youngsters who accommodated well to the slower students, and I had no friction there. The class was small in the beginning, and several of them dropped out during the year. Along toward spring, the feeling of the class degenerated to a sharp hostility. I could not account for this feeling, although I tried very hard. Finally, one day, when the hostility broke out in open rebellion, I lashed out at the students saying, "What's happened in this class? You used to be so much fun to teach and now the warm feeling is gone. Why?" They told me without difficulty.

This class developed much of its content material through group activity—such as small-group discussions, and group reports— partly because the students enjoyed it and partly to accommodate for the difference in performance levels of the students. The dropouts had left one group quite depleted. This group had requested a rearrangement of grouping, and I had denied the request because changing the groups after they have been established usually created much disturbance in a class. In this case, however, the entire class resented the fact that this group couldn't function with only three members, one of whom was frequently absent. With the class seeing the need, I had no problem changing the groups to a more balanced number, and we went back to the same pleasant warm relationship that had characterized the class in the beginning of the year.

One can see from the above class personalities that the collective personality is very much a function of the individuals that comprise it. In the creative class, the people who were not naturally creative responded to the stimulation of those who were, and the complexion of the whole group became creative. The lack of unity which characterized the second class came from the absence of response. Students in that class brought their problems to the classroom in a strike against living that deadened the natural impulses toward excitement which arose. In the eruptive class, the excitement generated from one central source, and the sparks spread all around the room. On days that the girl who was the source was absent, the class functioned differently. The polite class was almost all girls from upper-middle-class families who had taught them to be agreeable. The grouping on the basis of choice in the pleasant class gave everyone a comfortable place in the universe of the classroom, and the wide diversity of ability levels was shadowed by the common need of belonging.

THE OUTSIDE SEEPS IN

Although teachers must respond differently to each group that they meet even while they maintain many lines of consistency, they must also accommodate to factors outside the classroom which students bring in with them. Experienced teachers learn to prepare for seasons of stress. Everyone gets tense at the end of a grading period, and on the day report cards come out one might as well plan to talk about them because that is what the students are going to be thinking about regardless of the subject of the discussion. The day before a holiday is electric, and even Fridays are bad. I recall vividly a day that illustrates this kind of influence:

A lesson that in previous years had been vital seemed to go nowhere. The first-period class assembled late because of homeroom business, and when the students arrived in class they wouldn't settle down. They buzzed with their neighbors at every opportunity; they were poorly prepared with their assignments; they were unresponsive to the challenge the lessons posed; and I wound up doing most of the talking. The bell was a relief to all, and I tried to plan a better start for the next class.

Second period was worse than the first. The group of boys in the back who usually sat in sodden silence kept popping off to each other. Nobody in the class seemed to get the point of the lesson at all. This was a review lesson, and I had a sinking feeling that we had washed nine weeks of work down the drain as far as usefulness of the material was concerned. Accustomed to failure with that class, however, I relaxed with pleasure as the third one came streaming in.

This was the worst of all. Holding the reins was always difficult here because the students were so lively and so interested. Today was pandemonium. Not only were the classmates noisy, but they also ignored the lesson. After repeated attempts to settle their attention, I became exasperated. "What on earth is the matter with the classes today?" I asked. "They have been like this all day."

"The grading period is ending," they told me matter-of-factly, "and Monday starts the beginning of our last quarter."

This was true. Because spring vacation was starting in the middle of the following week, our break in subject matter would come then. The grades were ready, but I did not realize that students even knew the grading period had ended, and I was expecting this kind of behavior the following week on the day before vacation.

School activities also play a heavy role in the classroom. Prom fever breaks out a full week before the prom, and in this school, the senior-class play invaded the classroom a full month before curtain time. Football heroes sometimes feel they should be excused from Friday tests on the day of an important game.

World crises which occurred during my teaching years are unforgettable experiences because I lived through them with youth who were sensitive to the potency of these world affairs in their essentially yet-to-be-lived lives. Several examples follow:

I listened to the countdown for the first space flight with a class of all seniors. Throughout the program which was coming to us over the PA, the students gave absorbed attention, and when the countdown ended and the rocket soared, we soared with it in a pitch of excitement that took us worlds away into the future when space flight will shape a world we can't begin to predict. The situation is difficult to describe because what the students said or did was not important. What was important was what they were feeling, and they took me with them all the way.

The Cuban crisis was a nightmare. The morning after the President's announcement containing the ultimatum to Russia to withdraw her missiles from Cuba, our principal came on the PA and announced, in a wavering voice, that we would have an air-raid drill and that all the students should go in the halls and stand with their faces to the wall. Nothing could have more effectively defined for the students the seriousness of our situation. High school students are mature enough to know how inadequate such a procedure would be, and panic followed. The philosophies of high school students are yet unformed, and the students needed to depend on adults for their poise. They so much wanted to live because they sensed that they had not yet had the opportunity to share in life's deepest experiences. Most of them could not sleep at night that week, and classes were a shambles. This seemed an appropriate time in my classes to discuss the hazards and fears that men have faced throughout human history.

Kennedy's assassination, a tragedy to the entire nation, was a gut-grabbing experience for youth. While we were waiting after the initial announcement of the shooting, hoping the tragic end would not occur, girls sobbed openly and boys sat staring into space. We had a shift of classes, and when the final death announcement came, another hour of school faced us. The event seemed like the end of the world to the students. They were so upset they didn't even try to talk to each other. They simply sat immersed in grief so deep that they were almost in a state of physical shock.

My class was scheduled for a test, and the students took it when I said, "The greater the tragedy in life, the more important it is for us to do the next thing that needs to be done." When the class reassembled, I asked them whether or not they wanted me to count the test. After some discussion, they decided that they did. So I counted it, thinking as I did so, "Who dares to claim our youth are degenerate?"

As we see that students confined in the cages of the classrooms find varied climates depending upon the personality of the teacher, the aggregation of the students, and external factors which penetrate the classroom, we can begin to sense why they feel caged. They are there because society demands their attendance rather than because they want to be there, and they have little choice about what happens within the cage. Thus the taming begins.

CHAPTER FOUR

They Cringe

DISCIPLINE

"In an ideal, successful class, students learn and think. Order is kept and the teacher is in charge. However, this is not often the case. A good deal of what takes place occurs because a teacher can or cannot keep discipline," writes Sara Eaton, a senior.

In much the same manner that animals in a cage cringe when they hear the tamer crack the whip, students react to discipline in school. At times, teachers feel that the school system is little more than an expensive baby-sitting organization in which the foremost responsibility of the school is to keep youngsters off the streets, out of trouble, and out of the labor market from 8:30 to 3:30, 180 days of the year.

This feeling results from the fact that administrators cannot get rid of undesirable students. They can go through the gesture of expelling students, but if a parent makes an issue, the student is usually reinstated. The reason for this, of course, is because a youth has no constructive area of functioning in our society outside of school, and he is likely to remain a burden to society throughout his life without the training school can give.

The effect of this on the school, however, is overpowering. This supervision of youth is necessary and vital to our society, but the fact that the schools must do it is the basis of much of the problem of discipline in our public schools today. If students were only in school because they wanted to learn, the picture would be vastly different. As it is, discipline is little more than whipcracking.

Discipline is a necessary ingredient of any classroom. A classroom out of control is chaos, and the students, although they cause the confusion, resent its effect more than anyone else when such a situation develops. If a group gets far enough out of control, the situation can be physically dangerous with boys pushing each other through the windows or fighting. Such a classroom is likely to be destructive to property as well. Books, papers, even chairs have been known to come tumbling out of third-story windows in our school. The greatest damage of all, however, is to the personalities involved. The teacher loses his self-respect, and the students lose the desirable elements of their interaction.

Usually, however, disruptive behavior in the high school classroom is less obstreperous than it is in the earlier years of school. Students of high school age have developed a level of self-control in which the show-off has learned to raise his hand even though it may be waving almost constantly. Because the physical restlessness of puberty has calmed down, most of the students can sit still when they try, and whispering is now talking, every chance the students get, but talking which will quiet down upon command.

Most disruptive behavior in high school is underground. At this age, things fly through the air only when the teacher's back is turned. A student is more likely to leave an obscene note around the classroom than to make silly faces to get attention. Sleeping, daydreaming, writing notes, or doing homework for another class are various techniques which students use to escape boredom, and they are more likely to escape than to disrupt. Although talking is by far the most frequent disruption, gum chewing, arriving late to class, and finding excuses to get out of the classroom are some of the minor irritations that interfere with the learning process.

A student describes a disorderly situation as follows:

> Homeroom. I chose this intentionally though not a period room as I was not familiar with it 'til I entered this school. The 12 minutes in there are sometimes like hell and it is even worse when homeroom is extended. The bell has rung the third time but some students just won't bother going to their seats but instead are joking, yelling, and screaming. Our young teacher has a hard time as it is and for her remain only to seize strict measures. The troublemakers are often locked out.
>
> Finally everybody is in and everything is quiet. Just for a minute, 'til the pledge is over, but then the theatre starts over again. Girls are embarrassed, chewing gum heard, chairs removed, seats changed and the announcements disregarded.
>
> The dismissal bell hasn't even rang but a wild herd of students blocks the door almost killing each other in the competition who is first out. An unorganized bunch of youngsters. Homeroom. Let's hope it will change. My comment, "I doubt it."

Most situations are not this bad, but every teacher has to struggle with control.

THE BIG WHIP

Control of the classroom rests basically on the threat system. No matter how skillful the teacher or how cooperative the students, everyone knows that reprisals are possible. Here the administration provides one of its most important functions to the school. Hamstrung as administrators are with policy regulations, they do hover effectively in the background to keep this threat alive.

I don't know concretely how they do it. They walk threateningly but swing a little stick. They feel they can't expel a student, although they can threaten expulsion. Suspension is possible, but they use this wisely with reservation because it just gives a student a vacation from an unpleasant situation and, except for the aura of disgrace that surrounds it, is more a reward than a punishment. Administrators can't use physical punishment because that is against the law.

I do know something of their techniques. One of them is to listen. The student has a chance to present his point of view, and although guidance and discipline are supposed to be two different functions performed by different individuals in the system, the disciplinarians wind up serving important guidance functions. The primary responsibility of the vice-principal is to back the classroom teacher. The teacher has to win—the vice-principal knows this, and the student knows it—but the listening process helps the student realize it, and this sometimes helps.

One technique that's used is the waiting game. A student who is sent down for discipline cannot come back to class until the vice-principal admits him with a note. I have seen students sit that class hour every day for a week waiting to see the vice-principal, and this has an important psychological effect. By the time a student gets into the office for the conference, he is often ready to go back and behave. The waiting game gives some students a good chance to review the situation, and for the tough customer it's a good technique because to him waiting is such a boring process.

Although I have never witnessed a session where anger is used, I've heard descriptions of some that indicate this is a powerful force in a disciplinarian's office. Our vice-principals vary in their ability to command this technique, but each of them has adequate skill. The kind of anger that works is not a temper tantrum, but a constrained force that spells for the student an emotional comprehension of the evils of his ways. I have seen the effect of this on the students when they return to class, and this effect is helpful in behavior control.

In order to command the help of the big whip, the teacher must identify the culprit and describe the offense on the back of the slip he sends down to the vice-principal with the student. By the time students are finishing their high school years, they are quite skillful at disguising their activity, which makes this difficult. This is the reason why a teacher is reluctant to turn his back on a class. The moment he turns his back on some classes, the action begins. I would far rather leave a class of this sort unattended than turn my back on them, because students feel responsible for their own behavior when the teacher is gone. The general attitude of most of the class will help control those who feel frisky. When a teacher's back is turned, however, the situation becomes a contest with student against teacher, and the other students will sit back and observe with amusement the action of those who are taking advantage of this opportunity to misbehave.

Even though the system of the big whip is not always easily available, the administrators deserve much credit for the quality of their hovering. Their task is not an easy one, but it is vital. Because the student body comes from a variety of backgrounds, no blackboard jungle exists in the school. Although the discipline problems are not so great here as they are in some areas, they could be much worse if the threat system did not work so effectively. It is far from perfect, but it is firm.

LITTLE WHIPS

Experienced teachers seldom need to use the big whip because they soon learn to settle most behavior problems in the classroom. Here the most difficult situation to control is one in which a tacit cooperation among various members of the class develops and small explosions occur in various areas making it impossible to pinpoint the action. The only technique I ever found to deal with this was to put the class to work writing. This has a calming effect because it reduces the interaction between students and gives the teacher an individual approach through the papers they write. This process is, in a sense, group punishment, but in spite of frequent admonitions from the administration to the contrary, group punishment is sometimes justified. The hidden will of the class encourages disruptive action at times, and only punishing the entire class will change the will.

When individuals are concerned, grades are, of course, one of the mediums a teacher uses to control classroom behavior. Few teachers baldly state, "I'll lower your grade if you misbehave," but in practice grades are far more a measure of conformity than a measure of achievement. Most teachers try to state the grading policy early in the school year so that the student will know what is expected of him in the class. The overall grading policy of the school is broad enough to allow the teacher a wide latitude in determining his own practices. My grades were based on three areas: tests, homework, and classwork. The tests were, as far as possible, a measure of the factual knowledge the student had acquired, but both the homework and the classwork grades depended on how much the student conformed to my demands. The homework grade was fairly objective because it was based on the proportion of work done that had been assigned with some measure of quality of that work included. The classwork grade, however, was highly subjective and was influenced to some extent by the behavior of the student in the classroom. Although it was not always clear to the students that acting up in class would show up in grades, behavior counted.

Grades, however, were not very helpful in solving my discipline problems mainly because students apt to cause difficulty are not much interested in grades. Since almost no one needed the credit they earned in my course to graduate, the only way I could keep this group as working members of the class was to trick them into passing for the first term so they would become interested as a matter of pride in passing for the year. If the student could pass tests, this was a fairly easy situation because he had to come regularly and pay fairly close attention to what was happening in class in order to pass tests without doing the homework he so abhorred. If he couldn't pass tests, then I had to work hard to wring a passing homework grade out of him, and I was not likely to fail him because of misconduct in class. I was able to maintain high standards for high grades in my course, but the standards for passing were very low, and the students with discipline problems were generally in the low bracket.

Some teachers develop skill in using sarcasm simply to gain classroom control. If a teacher can't be clever about sarcasm, it is better to let it alone because it can easily be more degrading to the teacher than to the student. The closest I dared come to this sort of thing was to appeal to the sense of maturity that stirs in the breasts of most high school students. If a group of boys started tossing paper wads in the rear of the room, I might look at them in amazement and declare, "I was under the impression that this is a *high* school classroom!"

If the class laughed in response to such a statement, the effect was good. The boys were embarrassed and retired into their shells, but depending too much on this type of control provides an unpleasant atmosphere in the classroom that tends to spread to all the relationships eventually. Sarcasm can achieve effective immediate results, but its long-term effect is damaging, and a wise teacher uses it sparingly.

Although good honest anger is more desirable, about the worst thing a teacher can do is to lose his temper in front of a class. The students enjoy the show when this happens and plan ahead to create new crises and prolong the drama. Controlled anger, however, when it is justified, can draw lines beyond which students will not step and provide a clear atmosphere for work. This can best be expressed by a look, at most a few words spoken firmly. I almost never used this in my classroom because in my beginning days, when I needed it most, I didn't know how. After I gained enough skill in teaching to understand how to use it, I had other techniques I preferred. It inserts an element of fear in the classroom atmosphere that is contrary to the relaxed feeling I needed to make my room the laboratory of human relations I sought to achieve.

Various kinds of penalties are also a part of the threat system. A rule that students must have twenty-four hours notice before they can be required to serve detention was a great deterrent to the use of detention as a penalty. This rule exists because 75 percent of the students ride a school bus to school and supposedly need to have an opportunity to provide their own transportation home. This makes detention more effort than it is worth because the teacher not only has to remind the student the second day, but also has to be willing to follow through when the student doesn't show up. He won't the first time because the students try customarily to ignore a detention notice. Furthermore, a detention requires the teacher's time as well as the student's, and although the teachers must be on duty thirty minutes after classes are dismissed, they frequently have responsibilities outside the classroom that make detention supervision inconvenient.

This situation is unfortunate because detention can be a constructive relationship between student and teacher. It provides an opportunity for individual interaction which can lead to better understanding on the part of both parties involved. In the formal class relationship, students sometimes lose sight of the fact that teachers are human beings with needs and interests not too different from their own. In a personal discussion with no one else around, the student often sees a teacher in an entirely different light, and this understanding can give him an impetus toward self-control, which can be helpful. The few times I succeeded in using detention as a punishment, I invariably gained an understanding of the problems which the student had that could not have been revealed in more public surroundings. Even so, I seldom made the supreme effort required to force a student to serve detention.

Some teachers still use the grade school penalty of writing fifty, one hundred, or a thousand times, "I will behave in class," or some such statement. Although this keeps the student contained during the writing period, it is doubtful if such a penalty has any desirable long-term effect. If one is striving to get students to act more maturely, a childish task is not likely to achieve that end.

Some penalties fit the crime. Forcing students to pick up papers strewed around the room before the class can leave seems legitimate to me. If a class gets too noisy in group activity after one warning, sitting in heavy silence until the bell rings has a long-term quieting effect on future sessions.

Ingenuity in penalties does not always pay off:

One time, in my substitute days, I had a double section of boys in a shop class that I could not settle long enough to teach them a thing. After I had been working a month, the other classes had reached a functioning stage, and I was determined to conquer this challenge. When the class assembled, I waited for the first explosion and then ordered them all on their feet. We did calisthenics. After about fifteen minutes of vigorous action, I seated the students and started directions for the craft project I wanted them to undertake. When someone popped off, I hauled the class back on its feet to continue the calisthenics, and this continued until almost the end of the hour. Just as everyone was tired enough to sit down and listen, one boy ripped the middle seam of his pants from the stem to the stern as he bent over for the last toe-touching I had planned to use. I sent him to the office with a sweater tied around his waist to protect his modesty. When he returned laughing, the entire class was off again. Shall we say I tried?

The threat system, from the vice-principal down to the ingenuous classroom teacher, is a necessary part of the discipline program in any school in which education is a problem instead of a privilege. This is not, however, the only basis of discipline because two positive forces function to make self-discipline the most important basis of control. These are public opinion and respect.

HERD ACTION

The students themselves provide a body of public opinion within the classroom that directs the behavior of the students. Some classes maintain a high level of control, and others provide sanctions for disorder instead. This depends, of course, upon the composition of the class. When classes are sectioned according to ability level, one of these variables is clearly the social level of the students in the class. A student paper makes this point poignantly:

> I believe one can find certain similarities in classes
> which have bright or slower children. From my
> own experience, I can truly say that my slower class
> in geometry of tenth grade in no way compared to
> my very good class in English. I certainly do not
> believe one should judge on outward appearance only,
> but appearance is seemingly an insight to a person.
> In general the geometry class students were poorly
> dressed, not too well scrubbed, and very ill-mannered
> people. It was a terrible class and the behavior
> problem is something I cannot describe. I was in this
> class because I was poor in mathematics, but I
> do not consider myself an incorrigible. Truly,
> some of those people were.
> My English class, on the other hand, was a
> pleasure to be in. The students were nicely dressed,
> of above average performance in the class and most
> of all, they were well-mannered.

Individuals within the class strongly influence the tone of the public opinion. A student who brings a problem to class with him may be lifted out of his mood by the movement of the class or may find enough chords of discontent among the members of the class to carry it down with him. These elements stem from several sources.

Students bring their family problems to school, and these problems often erupt into problems of behavior in the classroom that influence others. During the course of the year, I came to realize that the days when Linda sat in the back of my classroom telling her neighbor what a terrible class this was had been preceded by horrible nights with her father, who was dying of cancer. Becky's constant eruptions in the classroom echoed the fights she had heard before she came to school that morning between her mother and her third stepfather because this marriage, too, was cracking. Jim would lose a fight over the use of the car at home and come to my class where he would pick a fight he could win.

Students bring their own problems to the classroom also. Broken romances, splintered friendships, just plain ego slippage when a student's grades are low or he didn't make the team or she didn't get invited all stalk the classroom. A classroom is an area for mending broken egos—a workshop where the teacher is a tool—and many of the discipline problems in the classroom stem from these ego needs. To some students, any kind of attention is better than none.

Many students just plain hate school, especially boys. Too often boys, because of their slower-maturation pattern, start school before they are ready, and unsuccessful experiences in the very beginning of their school careers set the foundation for this pattern of hate that builds through the years to a solid wall of rejection. Trapped by law and custom in this cage of hate, they sit. The obvious discipline problems they create during the junior high years reach deeper now, and their misbehavior is subtle and often vicious when it strikes. It shows itself mainly by refusal to participate in class activity, but blossoms out in any opportunity to sway others toward breaking up classroom activity.

Joe was an example of this:

Joe's father had died at sea in World War II. Handsome, dynamic, charming, Joe hated school, and his favorite pastime was leading the students in criticism of me. Often his starting point was test questions, and after he had argued through half a dozen of those, the entire class would be a little uneasy about the test. He even went so far one day as to accuse me of being a brainwasher.

"You are a dangerous influence in the school," he claimed.

He was referring to a lesson we had recently had about making decisions. I had boldly proclaimed, "When you make a decision you should stick to it, even if it is wrong." This had stirred an active discussion, and I thought we had a good lesson. In rebuttal to Joe's flagrant statement above, I said, "I didn't say anyone had to agree with me. I just said that was what I believed."

"But too many students accept what is told them without thinking it through," he countered.

Of course, there was enough truth in his argument to stir the class, although he was never able to undermine seriously the respect the students had for me. I could have squelched him easily because he frequently verged on rudeness, but his criticism was useful to the class and helped keep him a participating member of the group. Such action did not, however, make it easy to keep the class under control.

Sometimes, when a large number of psychological dropouts gather in a single class, teaching is almost impossible. I had a class like this once. Although the students did not get out of order too much, they refused to respond to any activity in the classroom. A vivid memory of one class session demonstrates this:

One of the few things that seemed to create interest was a thinkathon, a nondirective discussion. I sat with the students and when someone had something to say, he stood and said it. When he finished, he sat down and whoever wanted to speak next could rise and have the floor. Sometimes we used a general topic as the basis of discussion; sometimes we had a number of questions on the board from which the students could draw at will; and sometimes a class would prefer no direction at all. This class had never sparkled with thinkathons, but they had enjoyed them more than other kinds of activity. On this particular day, along toward spring, we had a series of questions on the board as the basis of our thinkathon. One student rose and made a brief comment about one of the questions and sat down. No one else moved the entire hour. Because of some rules that went along with the thinkathon, this hour was heavy. Talking to a neighbor or doing any kind of work at your seat meant a trip to the vice-principal. The public opinion of the class came through to me quite forcibly during that hour, and we had no more thinkathons.

Some students have basic personality qualities that make control difficult. The extrovert in my third class was one:

Diane was a beautiful, warm, outgoing individual who constantly broke out in spite of obvious efforts at self-control. She was the center of the eruptive class and constantly exploded with ideas without being recognized by the chair. Her fellow students responded to her vitality with constant whispering to each other and interruptions of their own. Although I frequently had to bring the class to order, I did it with willing patience because the disorder was participation rather than rebellion. I enjoyed the class, but it was not an easy group to steer.

One day one of the boys challenged Diane. "I'll bet you couldn't keep your mouth shut for the rest of the hour if you tried," he declared.

"I can so!" she insisted, and she sat for the remaining ten minutes without opening her mouth. This was a struggle though, and she almost slipped twice, reaching the pose of speaking and then remembering. We all enjoyed the experiment.

A disciplined classroom is not necessarily a quiet one. A class can be a din of noise and motion without chaos. The difference lies in the relationship of the students to the teacher. If the noise is created to taunt the teacher, the behavior is basically destructive; if the noise is interaction for achieving classroom goals, the behavior is basically constructive.

THE PEDESTAL

The most important of these qualities is self-confidence. Students spect the students have for the teacher. Some respect automatically accrues because the teacher is an adult, but most of the respect has to be earned. Several personality characteristics a teacher may develop have high value in earning this respect.

The most important of these qualities is self-confidence. Students can tell by the way a teacher walks into the room whether or not he knows what he is doing. Because this self-confidence has to be gained through experience, this technique is not much help to a beginning teacher. It consists of a manner that implies that the teacher expects the students to behave.

A second quality is dignity. A teacher does not have to be formal all the time, but he must have self-control and poise. I made the mistake when I first started teaching of thinking that I had to act angry when students misbehaved in order to get them back in line, and I went storming around the classroom stirring up great commotion.

An interesting demonstration of the effect of dignity or lack of it occurred once when my co-worker was out for an extended period of time, and I was trying to help the substitute:

> We had planned to unite our classes in the band room down the hall to hear a speaker from Alcoholics Anonymous. The absent teacher who had arranged for the speaker had assured me that he would speak all six periods (an unusual courtesy). Discovering at the last minute that the band had to use the band room that day because of a program scheduled in the auditorium, the substitute and I, after a hasty conference, decided we could jam both classes in his room by seating students on tables and standing some along the walls. This we did quite successfully for the first hour while we listened to a stimulating speaker describe his experiences with the AA program.
>
> At the end of the hour, the speaker put his coat on and prepared to leave. "But we have five more classes!" I exclaimed.
>
> "Oh, I couldn't do it again," he replied. "I wouldn't be able to distinguish what I'd said the first hour and what I'd be saying this hour. Besides, I have a business appointment."
>
> Sadly we watched him leave as the second-hour classes squeezed in. I had a lesson I could pull out of the file on alcoholism to fill the gap, but I could not leave the substitute stranded without a lesson plan for the day.
>
> "I'll get my folder on alcoholism and teach both classes this hour," I suggested. "You listen to me, and then you can use my materials and what you remember from the speaker and teach both groups next hour."
>
> He agreed, and when I returned to the room with my materials, I found the room in chaos. The conditions could hardly have been worse. The students were jammed together and greatly disappointed at not hearing the speaker. Of course, the day was also dark and drizzly, and every sound was magnified.
>
> Summoning my forces to control the group, I rose to full stature, put on a cold dignified stare, and said in a low and firm voice, "May I have your attention, please?" As I was waiting for the silence to grow from the front of the room where the students could see and hear me to the back of the room, the substitute teacher bellowed out from the rear of the room, "Shut up and quiet down!"
>
> It was just like dropping a bomb in the room. The students were off on a mad scramble of outshouting each other because they couldn't be heard.

All I could do was laugh when I realized how much I had learned about achieving control in a classroom. If one must be heard, whisper. Dignity is, indeed, an important element in control.

A third quality is patience. A class needs a little time to focus its attention, and if a teacher tries to move the students into order too rapidly, he is implying to them that their disorder is deliberate rather than natural, which is an admission of lack of control on his part. So what if he does have to speak to the students three times instead of once? That just means their personal interaction was absorbing and therefore valuable. Of course, there is a limit to how far this patience should go, but some of it is important. Patience with individuals who stir a class is also necessary because the more disruptive they are, the greater their individual adjustment problem is likely to be. Although the teacher's responsibility is to the whole class and thirty-four other students' time is being wasted, some patience with these individuals can provide for a better long-term adjustment.

Courtesy is another important quality. What we are in a classroom is so much more vital than what we say that teachers cannot expect courteous treatment from students whom they treat otherwise. "Quiet down," is much more desirable than, "Shut up." "May I have your attention, please?" is better than, "Attention, class!" Courtesy also involves such things as being willing to listen when a student has something to say and to dismiss the class as soon after the bell rings as the teacher can finish an idea. If a teacher respects the dignity of the students in his class, he is much more likely to receive courteous treatment from them.

A teacher must also be serious. If he is constantly stirring up the classroom with scintillating, sparkling conversation, he is likely to get more response that he can handle. This does not mean that he can never crack a joke if it is appropriate to some point being developed, but it does mean that the basic approach to learning should be serious. Some classes can take much more fun than others, and some teachers can take more active responses than others, but a certain amount of reserve is a valuable stabilizing factor in a classroom.

WHIP SKILLS

During the first week of school virtually no discipline problems appear. One might believe that the students had met for a conference and agreed, "We'll give him a chance to show us what he can do before we test him out." This doesn't occur, of course. It is likely that the students are not even conscious of this phenomenon. If they think about their behavior that week in any terms, they probably say to themselves, "I'm going to be good in school this year and do everything the teacher says."

Whatever the basis of it, this lull is important because it gives the teacher an opportunity to demonstrate to the students what he has to offer. "How does he grade?" "Is he interested in the material he is teaching?" "Does he know what he is doing as far as classroom operation is concerned?" "How much homework does he require?" "Does he know what he is talking about?" All these questions are important in a student's evaluation of a teacher. The teacher has an opportunity to prove himself on these points before the discipline problems start. If he passes this scrutiny in a positive manner, he is unlikely to have many serious discipline problems because when students respect a teacher for his teaching ability, they seldom bother to misbehave.

Sometime along about the second or third week, testing begins. Some brave soul acts up, and the students observe with interest how the teacher responds. They have no respect for a teacher who cannot handle discipline problems, and the teacher sets the tone for the level of discipline that he expects to maintain within the class for the year at this point. Most teachers start out tougher than they are likely to remain through the year, relaxing the standards as they develop closer personal ties with the students.

Some quite simple techniques help when these problems start. A teacher must be firm. Disciplining is not a pleasant responsibility, and a teacher cannot be nice about it. If a student is disturbing the class, the teacher is responsible for stopping him. He must control his anger, but he needs also to be honest in his anger when it is deserved. If a teacher insists that all his relationships with youth must be pleasant, he should get out of teaching.

A teacher must also be consistent. He must mean what he says and follow through with it. Of course, one should be careful what one says in the first place, but carrying through what one starts is also important.

One helpful device is to wait. If a student is whispering to someone next to him when the class is in action, just stand and wait. The students in the class will gradually become conscious of what the teacher is waiting for, and they will all look at the culprit. When he becomes aware of the fact that he is the focus of attention, he will retire into embarrassment, and the teacher doesn't need to say a word.

Sometimes just throwing a little weight around helps. If the class has misbehaved too many times during the hour to suit the teacher, he can hold the students after the bell rings. He simply says, when the students jump out of their seats and start out of the room, "The class has not been dismissed. No one will be excused until everyone is in his seat and quiet." This just takes a few seconds, and when the class does leave, the students go in an orderly fashion; they know that the teacher is in control of the class. They remember it the next day, too.

Whatever the source, the methods, or the reasons for discipline in a public school classroom, that discipline is a vital part of our educational system. Members of our society learn primarily in our schools that freedom does not mean license. Discipline in most modern American families has been softened with permissiveness. Rather than the authoritarian demands of the parents of yesteryear, families today are child-centered to the point that many children enter school with little or no skill for accepting controls on their behavior. By the time the students reach high school, they have learned to accept external controls, but the high school years are important ones in learning self-control and direction.

I always felt the best measure of my teaching was taken when I was not in the room. No administrator for whom I have ever worked ever approved of a teacher's leaving a class unattended, but I used to do it anyway. I felt that until I could leave a class alone and come back and find the students reasonably quiet and constructively occupied, they were not ready to graduate from high school. My room was in the catacombs, far from the beaten path, and I often thought how interesting it would be not to show up some day and see what would happen. If my door was unlocked, I honestly believe the administration would not know I was absent. My students would enter the classroom, take the roll, and wait awhile for me to come. If we were doing something they could carry on by themselves, they would proceed with the lesson, and if not, they would study or talk quietly among themselves. If this happened, it would be the greatest tribute I could receive as a teacher. To me, the goal of all discipline is self-discipline, and this is one of the most important responsibilities our educational system bears today.

Thus the taming progresses.

CHAPTER FIVE

They Jump

LEARNING PROCESSES

*"A classroom is a place of learning. It can be won-
drously interesting or drastically boring. Often times
the teacher makes the class interesting and often times
the pupils,"* writes Peggy Sorrel, a senior.

Education may sometimes be compared to training animals to jump through the hoop. The trainer carefully designs the behavior and rewards the animal when the objective is achieved. In our educational system, learning is generally directed to specific objectives, and the degree of achievement of those objectives determines the amount of the reward.

Such a concept of education, however, is narrow because the tamers are concerned with far more than fact stacking. Although they expect the animals to jump at the crack of the whip (tests), they believe that learning to jump makes the animals more effective in all aspects of living. One might think of education as a dual highway. One lane is fact stacking, the process of accumulating knowledge for use in the future. Most of the deliberate efforts of teaching go down this lane. The second lane is behavior changes in the individual which result from what the student is learning. Both lanes are important; both are occurring constantly to some extent; and in order to understand learning processes, one must keep both in mind.

Students are often critical of school because they see so little application of what they are learning to their actual lives. Although curriculum is molded to the past more than to the future and much of what they learn they'll never use, this criticism is not entirely just. Students seldom appreciated the factual value of the course I taught at the time they took it. My reinforcement came from alumni who almost invariably told me, "I didn't realize until after I left how much I would use the material I learned in this course."

In some areas, the criticism is entirely just. The following example happened to me before I started to teach regularly:

> I did remedial reading work. One of my students, although of at least average intelligence, was a sophomore in high school who tested in reading at a preprimer level. I went to the school to consult with his English teacher about what kind of work we could design for him.
>
> "We are studying Shakespeare," she declared.
>
> "Such reading scarcely seems reasonable for him," I replied.
>
> "But this is the only time in his life he will have an opportunity to get to know Shakespeare!" she argued.

BEHAVIOR CHANGES

Teachers seldom have an opportunity to observe behavior changes resulting from classroom experiences, but occasionally such opportunities arise, and when they do, they are a great satisfaction. The following incident is one which occurred in my classroom. In order to understand it, a brief background of one of the students is necessary:

Jerry was a good example of what is meant by "positive traits tend to go together." He was the captain of our county championship football team, a brilliant boy with blond curly hair, blue eyes, and a masculine profile. He was vice-president of the senior class and quite successful in everything he undertook.

I had been much disappointed in him as a student. He was in my homeroom his sophomore year at which time he had been president of the sophomore class. Being familiar with his extremely high test scores, I was disappointed when he proved to be an indifferent student. He was quite content with the gentleman's B (it has gone up from the C of yesteryear probably because of competition for college entrance) and did all his work with a minimum of bother. The work was good enough that I had no reason to complain, and this I could accept because life outside the classroom demanded much of Jerry, and the things he was doing were important. I was disquieted, however, by his quietude in class. Day after day he sat listening, volunteering nothing, and responding with a token answer when pressed. He had agreed with me when we were making New Year's resolutions that he should contribute more, but no change had occurred.

The incident happened in the third-period class during a lesson on complexes. In trying to illustrate the emotional nature of a complex, I said, "If you are prejudiced against something, reasoning about it doesn't change the way you feel. For example, you may be prejudiced against the color yellow. Some conditioned response learning may have occurred below the level of conscious thought. Perhaps a second-grade teacher wore a yellow blouse the day she taught you to hate school. It doesn't matter how much someone describes the virtue of yellow to you. You don't care if it is a bright color. So is red and that is what you see when someone tries to talk you into liking yellow."

The class sat blinking. Some were listening, but none were interested in what I had to say. They didn't even have their guard up because they hadn't yet suspected that what I was getting to was the fact that you can't talk people out of hating Negroes. I tried again, seeking an example that might stir them. "There are good complexes, too," I said. "I am absolutely unreasonable about the virtues of this school. I think it's great, and it doesn't make any difference how many football games we lose, I can find some excuse for it." This was working better. The class began to stir in their seats, and I pursued it further.

"I can sit back rationally," I said, "and recognize some of the faults of our school. It is too big. My students don't like to work. The bus lanes are dangerous. . . . But when I try to summarize these criticisms, I always conclude, 'but this school *is* the greatest!' "

Open laughter occurred in a few spots, and I rushed to capitalize on the interest aroused when suddenly from Jerry's quiet corner of the room, he reared up out of his seat without raising his hand and said, "Love can be a complex!"

I had never thought of it before, but what a profound concept he had stumbled upon! We did not discuss race prejudice that day. We talked about our own experiences of love and how irrational they can be. The students recognized this factor in their parents' relationship to them, realizing that this accounted to some extent for the fact that their parents so often expect more from them than they seem to be able to achieve, even when they try. They recognized that their early love relationships with members of the opposite sex contained this element too and that probably their girl friends and boy friends were not quite as wonderful as they seemed, except they still thought so because they had a complex. Planting such an idea in a classroom is like dropping a stone in a pool of water. The ripples widen and widen until they are lost in the mist.

This lesson marked a behavior change in Jerry. He became a part of that class in a way he hadn't been before, although he was still quiet most of the time. During the remainder of the year, he made other valuable contributions to the class and thought seriously about the work he was doing for it.

Sometimes behavior changes occur without the teacher being aware of them at all. At the conclusion of a courtship and marriage unit one year I asked the students to write at the end of the test paper what they had learned of value in the unit. One student who did not do at all well on the factual part of the test wrote, "I learned not to run away and get married. My boy friend wanted me to elope, and I would have done it if I hadn't been taking this class."

Some important behavior changes are unrelated to subject matter as such, but occur because of the classroom situation. The following incident is an example:

Once I asked a boy who used crutches to walk in my class to go to the board and write his answer as other students were doing. He couldn't believe at first that I meant to make him mount his crutches and walk in front of the class to make a mark on the board. As I and the class waited patiently, he slowly did so. When I saw him walking home that night, I realized what an important change in behavior was resulting from that walk to the board. For the first time he had accepted himself as a worthwhile person with paralyzed legs. The walk home was a long walk for him, but his shoulders were broad, and he could do it. He did not need to depend on others to get him home anymore.

Behavior changes are difficult to measure, but they are the most important part of education. Of the three areas of objectives defined in teacher training—attitudes, skills, and understanding—attitudes provide the basis of most behavior changes. Attitudes are emotional sets that serve as a springboard for action. A study of attitude change on integration as a result of social studies classes in our county showed discouraging results. Students' prejudices against Negroes remained so through several years of social studies classes, but such a test does not measure behavior change. The boy on crutches described above would probably evidence much prejudice on an attitude test. His parents, divorced, were Southern and not wealthy, and generally these people are more rabid in their discontent. Their child would reflect their views. In face-to-face relationships, however, this student would be more likely to accept Negroes as worthwhile people than he would if he had not learned to accept himself.

Behavior changes in skills are quite apparent. My students made discernible progress in creating bulletin-board displays, drawing and interpreting graphs, writing scientific experiments, presenting oral reports, and writing in general. Skills are relatively easy to teach because they are tangible and the practice of them is a participating process.

ACCUMULATING KNOWLEDGE

Fact stacking is like shoveling smoke. Encountering a sense of vagueness prevalent in a class carefully trained a month previously on a given concept is disturbing. To illustrate specifically:

I used the process of cracking codes as the basis of teaching the steps involved in the scientific method. The students often became quite involved with this lesson, and at the end of the hour they could usually identify five steps. By Friday, when we had our weekly quiz, about three-fourths of them were likely to remember these five steps, but when we had our unit test several weeks later, only about half of them could answer correctly multiple-choice questions dealing with them. This lesson was basic to much of what we did in the course, and when we needed to refer to these steps at various points in the curriculum development, I might boldly pick a student and say, "John, what is the first step of the scientific method?"

A blank silence would hit the room.

"I don't remember," he might finally reply.

"Who can?" I would ask.

Silence. Then a timid hand might appear in the distance and some brave student would take a guess. Gradually, by pooling all their knowledge and eliminating the errors, we reconstructed the picture and went on.

Exposure to facts is no guarantee that the facts will "take," and we know as we teach that most of the facts the students do learn will be forgotten. Yet fact stacking is important, too. Not only is the accumulated knowledge useful, but also the process of trying to accumulate knowledge produces the behavior change.

The course I taught was an unusual one, being a composite of material from several areas of social science, and we had no standardized achievement test available with which to measure the number of facts the students were learning. I did, however, use the Engle Achievement Test, a standardized test designed for high school psychology, at the beginning and end of the year. Even though this test was no measure of the total process in my course, it demonstrated some gain in knowledge of the psychology we studied. The results from one year are shown in the accompanying graphs. The picture when broken down by average percentile points gained by each class refers to the classes described in Chapter 3.

METHODS

The classroom is a fifty-five-minute challenge, reduced to fifty minutes by the mechanics required to keep a classroom going. Educators developed this length of period originally with the idea of giving students an opportunity for supervised study in the class-room, and it works very well in some classes. In math the length of the period gives ample opportunity to check homework, present a

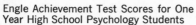

Engle Achievement Test Scores for One
Year High School Psychology Students

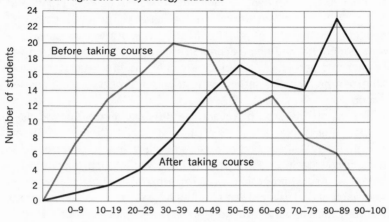

Average Improvement by Class on Engle
Achievement Test for High School Psychology

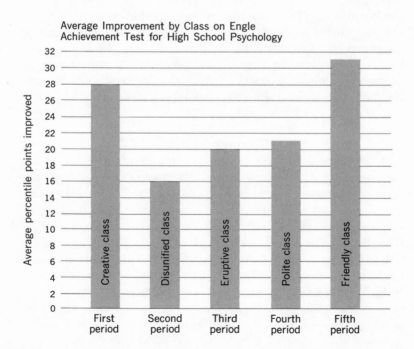

new concept, and practice it in class so the teacher can determine whether or not a student understands it well enough to practice at home. Activity classes thrive on the long period. The bother of changing clothes for physical education is more worthwhile with a long period. Art and home economics classes can accomplish a full project in a period. Long periods are valuable in a laboratory where an experiment can be set up, carried out, and written up in one fell swoop.

For many classes, however, the fifty-five-minute period is a burden. For subjects like English and social studies, a fifteen-minute interval at the end of a period is just time to get oriented in a homework task, and students tend to waste such opportunities. When we had short-period days for athletic events, which meant that each period was cut ten minutes to make an hour at the end of the day, most teachers found they accomplished as much as they did on regular days.

Teachers use a variety of methods of instruction to fill this fifty-minute challenge. Actually, changes of activity within a given hour ease the strain on both teacher and student. An excellent teacher claims, "I have very few discipline problems, and I attribute this partly to the fact that I am sensitive to rising restlessness among my students. I frequently use a change of pace. When the class comes in there may be a contest on the boards, a student quiz on my desk, a writing assignment on which I can draw, and a discussion question from which I will stray without a feeling of guilt. I am a master at getting off the subject."

SPOTLIGHT ON THE TEACHER

Most high school classes (I would guess about 80 percent) are teacher-centered in their operation. The teacher may lecture; the teacher may present a series of concepts and raise discussion questions based on them to allow student participation; the teacher may raise discussion questions on textbook assignments or draw from the students' own experiences as the basis of discussion. Sound reasons account for this procedure, although methods books decry too much dependence on it. A teacher may prepare such lessons with reasonable ease, and if the material is vital and relevant to the students' needs, students gain benefit from such procedures. Also the class is easier to control, and subject matter develops in an organized fashion, making it possible to cover curriculum required in the amount of time allotted.

Some teachers do give long, boring, dry lectures, but these are not the good teachers; and they don't lecture all the time, or they wouldn't survive. Some good teachers, however, use the lecture method quite extensively. "Sometimes," one of the best teachers in our school remarked, "there isn't any way to get an idea across except to tell the students what you want them to know." A student describes her class as follows:

> During my junior year I attended one of the finest planned courses I had ever taken. I truly learned more than just what was in my textbook and yet I was never over-burdened with homework. Not only did the student have to be prepared for each period but the teacher also had a carefully worked out schedule of the hour; what she would say, the questions she would ask, and the major and minor points she planned to bring out and emphasize.
>
> Each student received a detailed outline of what the grading period contained. The student was expected to be prepared each day by reading a specified amount of material. This only consisted of a few pages from the text equalling no more than a half-hour of reading and studying each evening. Every two weeks the students handed in a sheet of paper stating the extra reading done and a comment on it. Approximately a hundred pages extra reading was average.
>
> One day a week upon entering class we received a short quiz of five questions on the reading of the previous night. Then down to business. No notes were allowed to be taken. The teacher would lecture on the material we had had for homework. She brought out points the book had not mentioned, such as the results of a particular action or what caused this problem to become existent. (My teacher believed in discussing the feeling of the times and although dates were unimportant, the time period was extremely important.) She would ask the pupils questions which were not normally found in the reading matter but had to be evolved from common sense. At the end of each train of thought we were allowed to ask questions. Our teacher gave us three or four minutes at the end of the period to take notes.
>
> Although I learned a great deal by this method, I

remember the fear all of us felt once the lecture began.
Every time she asked a question my mind would go
blank. One dared not lose track of the train of thought
and questions asked for fear of being caught unaware.
One was always prepared for a lesson. Although no
specified amount of extra reading was required, each
person attempted to have about a hundred pages read
since this was what she expected. There could be no
doubt of the interest that this teacher took in her work
and in her students. I know she must have worked as
hard or harder than we did in preparing each day's
lesson, but she made it interesting and worthwhile.
I owe her much admiration and gratitude.

Some teachers are more skillful storytellers than lecturers. Students gain more than just satisfaction from listening to a teacher spin a yarn. Through the years the good ones collect anecdotal material that illustrates concepts needed in a manner that intrigues and informs simultaneously. I used to read to my students sometimes, especially in the nonacademic classes. Some of the stories I used so many times that I almost learned them verbatim, and they provided a basis of common experience that was emotional as well as intellectual. I tried tape recording one once when I was planning to use it five times the same day to avoid strain on my voice. The effect was lost, even though the students listened to the story and knew what it was about, because they missed the identification that develops when actual reading occurs.

Teachers also develop discussion questions that are so good they work year after year. One of my favorites, "If a student in this class were to be suddenly switched with a savage from the Congo, which would adjust better?" guaranteed a good discussion on the nature of intelligence, for example.

Students enjoy discussion classes, especially if the material discussed is a dialogue, i.e., an interchange of ideas and experiences rather than an examination of knowledge in which the teacher expects a right answer. Even though I considered my ability to develop good discussion classes my weakest skill in teaching, the students ranked discussions as contributing the most to their learning when I asked them to rank our various classroom procedures in order of merit. The problem of depending too much on discussion classes is that such discussions may descend to the level of what

I call "yak" classes. These are classes where students sit around and exchange ignorance. To make a discussion vital, the material must relate to the experience of the students, but often their experience is so limited that the discussion makes no progress in the development of new ideas.

SPOTLIGHT ON THE STUDENTS

Some classroom methods might be classified as student-centered. Panel discussions, oral reports, contests, small-group discussions, and student-directed discussions put the students in the spotlight rather than the teacher. Most teachers use some of these occasionally, but few do it with much skill. Panels are difficult to do well; oral reports generally are deadly. Contests are appropriate classroom activity in that they add an element of excitement and can change the pace effectively. Sometimes in an effort to encourage wider participation in discussion, teachers arrange the class in groups to allow five or six simultaneous discussions to occur. Student-directed discussions can be quite effective if the student in charge is skillful.

To be realistic, however, one must realize in developing student-centered classes that the students need opportunity to work at these skills before any of these methods are likely to be successful. Most students enter high school with little experience at taking the classroom spotlight, and just putting a student in front of the class is not enough. Patience, setting standards with the group, and evaluation of the degree to which these standards are achieved must be a part of the process with the class if student-centered activity is to succeed.

SPOTLIGHT ON ACTIVITY

A third group of learning processes might be classified as activity-centered. Minor subjects such as music, art, physical education, home economics, shop, typing, speech, dramatics, and journalism are all primarily activity-centered classes in which the student gains most of his knowledge from the doing rather than the saying. Of course, some theory is also included in most of these courses, but the emphasis is certainly on the activity. Some academic classes like math, business courses, science, and foreign languages are about half and half. That is, the principles learned are an integral part of the classroom process.

Other academic classes are only activity-centered if the teacher deliberately makes them so. These are primarily English and social studies. Movies are one type of activity-centered classroom procedure used in these courses. The use of movies in classrooms is of debatable value. On the negative side, movies are often of poor quality; the equipment for operating them does not always function properly; students tend to regard movies as a good way to kill time and don't take them seriously; and scheduling movies is so complicated that one cannot count on using them at the appropriate time. [1]

The many splendid films not available for school use make the ones available seem ridiculous, and often one must exercise ingenuity to capture value from the ones at hand. Once when we were using a very old film related to the problem of choosing a marriage partner, the class was scornful of the almost ankle-length skirts of the girls in the film. These students were much impressed, however, with the fact that the elements in choosing a marriage partner had changed little in the intervening years when they stopped to think about it.

Teachers can't be blamed for becoming discouraged with efforts to use films. The waste of time when the bulb burns out, the frustration of having a film arrive a week before the class is ready for that lesson because of the unending interferences from the operation

---

[1] Scheduling films in the school where I taught was a complicated process. The board of education had a film library, but in order to use one of their films a teacher had to order it weeks in advance. As the librarian in the school did the ordering, she had to have time to include a particular film in her regular schedule of orders; the materials center needed time to report the availability of the film; the film had to be sent on the pony express, which was an interschool delivery system in the county that saved money and wasted time. A rigid rule against picking up films from the center made circumvention of these delays impossible.

Films were available from the public library also, but this library had few films related to school use and enforced a rule that schools could not use any films which were also available in the board of education library. One could, however, pick up films personally which enabled one to get a film on fairly short notice if it happened to be in.

The third source was the state health department, which had a number of appropriate free films. Of course, the teacher had to pay the postage and insurance since there were no funds available in the school; and the use of these films meant a trip to the post office, a burden of time in a busy day. Even though the health service was most efficient, those films also had to be ordered months in advance because the demand for them was so great. However one scheduled films, the process was so complicated that a teacher found it easier to get along without them.

of the school, and the fight with a fellow teacher over the use of the projector often discourage a conscientious teacher.

Because some teachers use films to kill time, students expect them to be an entertaining device, and one often has difficulty molding films into effective learning experiences. During a mental health unit, I had a long series of films, each of which was selected for the development of a particular concept. In an effort to get students to write film reports so they could keep these factors sorted out for future use, I met with serious opposition from the students.

In spite of all these difficulties, teachers often use films. They offer a variation of classroom routine that can be quite stimulating; they serve as a means of making difficult points clear; they present a more direct experience with the subject matter than just talking about it can do; and they provide a common basis of experience for all the members of the class.

Another activity-centered method is the use of various drama techniques. Skits, role playing, and play reading added richness to my classes. At least one teacher in the county went even further than these informal types of drama and organized a drama troupe that learned parts and put on plays for his classes. One of my dreams was to use an accelerated group sometime to make a film-strip. Filmstrips are very useful in classroom procedure, and practically none are available in my subject area. Such a project could have much value both for the class producing it and for the classes observing it.

Bulletin-board construction was another activity-centered technique widely developed in my classes. Groups worked on them while the class proceeded with other business, but evaluations of them were important parts of class activity. Finding the meaning intended by the group who constructed the display often provided the basis of deeper understanding of the subject matter than other kinds of discussion could have achieved.

We also did many experiments, most of which we devised for ourselves on ourselves. Some time-tested experiments wore through the years, but quite interesting effects resulted from requiring groups to develop experiments for the class. Many of them produced little or no scientific evidence, but the exploratory approach added much vitality to the learning process.

Tests are also an important part of learning. If the students discover which answers are correct quickly, they learn many facts from taking tests. Students who usually sit quietly despite efforts to stimulate an argument as a basis of discussion will sometimes argue long and hard over an ambiguous test question. Preparing for tests often is an important review of material being covered that would be completely lost without the review. Discussing tests after they are returned fixes facts more clearly in mind.

Testing also helps a teacher do a better job. He must deal with concrete concepts that can be tested, and writing test questions forces a teacher to be analytical about the material covered. I tried to write one multiple-choice question each day before I started to teach the lesson we were having that day, and this helped me to clarify in specific terms an objective understanding for each lesson.

However, tests are also a difficult phase of teaching. Students worry about tests without doing much effective studying in preparation for them. For the teacher, administering them can be harrowing, and grading them time consuming and tedious. The dependence on objective-type testing in our system has created a type of education that deals with minutia rather than important broad concepts. "The world is a swirling mass of unrelated events," wrote a talented student, which is an accurate description of what students see when they look at education.

Although taking notes on content is a time-honored learning process, notebooks of high school students are more amazing than the contents of a woman's pocketbook. Boys, if they carry notebooks at all, usually have sparse ones, but girls' notebooks are so jammed with everything that locating fresh paper is a time-consuming and frustrating chore. Such a notebook is devoid of useful notes, and rarely does a student know how to take good ones. A new course called "Notehand," developed by the business department for college-bound students, did train a few in this skill, but not many.

Some classroom time is devoted to study. Teachers vary greatly in how much time is so invested, but all teachers use some of it for supervised study. Finding it was more profitable to use a full hour occasionally than to use short periods frequently, I usually had some research project for each unit which required classroom time for development. We also spent much of our study time in the library, since library experiences are increasingly important as knowledge accumulates and leisure time increases. Planning group activities and improving study skills were also classtime consuming.

Because teaching is an art, the best method in any classroom depends upon the teacher. Just as some artists work well with watercolors and are ill at ease with oil, some teachers stack well with teacher-centered techniques and stumble when the students take the center. The skill employed in a technique is far more important than which technique is used, although some variety is also important.

Training in a classroom is a dual-lane road, however, and the broader highway is open in classrooms when the head and the heart work together. The indifference of the second-period disunified class shows clearly on the achievement graph, but other things happened in that class that made it far from a failure. Stan, a psychological dropout, stopped smoking and started lifting weights to prove to me he was a man. Jane prevailed upon her father, a member of Alcoholics Anonymous, to address the class. He was a warm success with the students, and both Jane and her father gained stature from the experience. Becky broke off with her boy friend because she realized she was too serious too young and somehow blamed psychology class.

Education obviously does far more than jump the animals through the hoop. We must turn now to observe the human relationships involved if we are to understand fully the taming process.

CHAPTER SIX

They Paw

STUDENT–TEACHER RELATIONSHIPS

"The teacher doesn't like me," commented Carol Brady as she saw the C on her report card.

Always in the classroom the relationship between the student and the teacher plays a vital part in the educational process, especially the part involving behavior change. Most of the pawing is fun. Affectional relationships between teachers and students vary from casual pleasantries to deep concern, and they may be reciprocal relationships or one-way roads. They are the basis of most of the go-power in education both to the student and to the teacher. A teacher's influence on a student is important because it is sustained over a long period of time whether either of them likes it or not, because the teacher must judge the student and convey that judgment through grades, and because the teacher represents many things to the student. Pawing can hurt when claws are extended, and because of the nature of some of these representations, claws creep out.

CLAWING

To students, a teacher represents authority. Each classroom is autonomous because the teacher determines what happens in it, and he will receive the backing of the principal or even the board of education if challenged. At least, this is what the students believe, and usually this is true. A teacher must feel that the principal will support him in periods of controversy or nothing very important can transpire in the classroom. Principals do give direction to what a teacher may or may not do, but they must do this privately if the teacher is to function effectively.

This authority irks some students who resist it because they have not learned to adjust to it in other areas of their lives. Students with dictatorial parents are apt to rebel against the teacher's authority because they have had no opportunity to rebel at home. Students with easygoing parents often rebel against authority presented by the teacher because they haven't learned to accept it at all. All the students rebel against the authority some of the time, because this is part of the pawing process.

This rebellion takes many forms. Students sometimes go on a "sit-down strike." I invariably got a rash of this after a lesson on prejudice which involved a description of the vivid experience I had when I participated in the civil rights march on Washington. For students who have a prejudice against Negroes, this lesson probed a tender spot. Instead of speaking out in class to express their views, they quit working in class. Some students decide they don't like the teacher the first week of school and sit out the 180 days doing nothing.

Mike was an example of a student on a sit-down strike:

Not needing a psychology credit to graduate, he refused to take a test one day in late spring. Since students must take tests to stay in my room, I sent him to the vice-principal's office for discipline. At that time, students could not reenter the class until a parent contacted the teacher and made arrangements for the student's return.

When Mike's mother called me, she informed me that Mike didn't like my course. With a tight voice I replied, "Do you think Mike will be able to go through life without doing things he doesn't like to do?" She agreed that this was unlikely, and I agreed to readmit Mike to my class if she would persuade him to work when he got there.

Mike came back to class the next day and stayed ten minutes, long enough to refuse another test. The second step in our procedure was to suspend the student until the parents came to school for a conference with the teacher, the vice-principal, and the student. At Mike's conference, the vice-principal did all the talking. Although she used about thirty minutes' worth of words, all she said was that Mike had to stay in my class in order to stay in school, and if he didn't stay in school, he wouldn't graduate.

Realizing he had lost the battle, Mike turned to me and blurted, "Why do you write so small on the board?"

"I don't think I do write too small," I replied. "No one has complained."

The vice-principal grabbed this straw eagerly. "Have you had Mike's eyes tested?" she asked of the parents.

They had not. I offered to change Mike's seat to one nearer the board, but he refused because he did not want to leave the group of boys with whom he was seated. When his eyes were checked, he did need glasses, which he eventually got. After returning to class, he made feeble stabs at taking tests, but he waited until the final to reciprocate. This he took because he knew I would throw him out if he didn't, but he didn't read any of the questions. He just marked answers at random, and he failed the course—untamed to the end.

Sometimes, however, the pawing helps:

Gil went to the vice-principal once because when I told him to get to work on his vocational booklet, he replied with a sneer, "I ain't gonna do that stuff." In this case, the vice-principal gave him the works, and he came back to class subdued and asked for help in undertaking his notebook. Although angry and sullen, he did his work, and the first major test he had after that encouraged him because he made a C on it. After this, he did his work with even more care, but continued his unpleasant manner until the end of the year. The next winter, I saw him in the hall outside my class-room dressed in uniform and waiting to see me. His sullenness had turned to shyness—an important behavior change.

Students sometimes resist authority by becoming a discipline problem and "getting even" with the teacher by deliberately stirring up the class. This, of course, requires whipcracking, but it is easier to handle than the sit-down strike because the system is geared for it.

Sometimes students resist the authority of the teacher by appealing to their parents for help. This is rare because parents realize better than their children that they can't fight city hall, and they tend to avoid creating unnecessary animosity between their child and the teacher. If parents feel that a teacher has abused his authority and make an issue, the process usually creates tensions rather than dissolves them. If students do not like a teacher, however, the teacher is much more likely to be criticized if dealing with sensitive areas of subject matter such as sex education than if student-teacher relationships are generally good. Obviously the students know what to discuss at home and often protect the teacher by silence.

Sometimes students resist authority by trying to get a transfer. This is possible in the school, although not automatic, and most students believe it is difficult. If successful, the student has to face the same problem with the next teacher.

The teacher sometimes receives attacks stimulated by anger at someone else:

Once a student in one of my classes was having difficulty with the other students in his group over the construction of a bulletin board. Sometime during the hour, he threw my snow boots out the window. Students working on the bulletin boards during class have freedom to move about the room to gather materials, and he did this so slyly that no one realized it. Although I knew the group was having trouble, I did not realize its seriousness until I found my boots after a lengthy search after school. In this case, the student was not angry at me. He was angry at other members of his group, but he relieved his aggression by tossing *my* boots out the window.

Teachers carry the weight of many shortcomings they do not actually possess. Often students attribute their own shortcomings to the teacher. When a student says, "The teacher doesn't like me," what he means most of the time is, "I don't like the teacher." As students chatter about teachers, which they frequently do, one learns more about the personality of the student talking than the personality of the teacher he is describing.

CLAWING BACK

So far I have been discussing the teacher-pupil relationship as though it were a one-way road with the teacher standing like an automaton receiving the attacks without response. This, of course, is not the case.

One vicious occurrence is personality clashes. The first semester I taught I fell headlong into such an experience:

> All I remember about the student involved was that he had red hair, but I also remember that he never walked into my classroom after this clash developed without causing me difficulty. I, in turn, did everything wrong as far as he was concerned. We agreed at the end of the year that we were not good for each other, and this was the pleasantest way our relationship could have ended.

The next year when a particular student bothered me, I let him alone. I just said to myself, "I might as well accept the fact that I am not going to teach him anything and let him sit," which I did.

Many students through the years, I am sure, felt a personality conflict existed because I needled many of them, but if I didn't like them personally, I let them alone.

One needs to realize that these clashes are a function of the teacher's personality as much as the student's. Teachers vary in the qualities that disturb them. The quality that disturbed me so much was dishonesty. Some students would rather cheat than earn a grade honestly, and for some reason this quality bothered me more than some other faults that would concern other teachers more than me. I recall one student who copied homework, cheated on tests, and even went so far as to turn the same book report in to me three times. Realizing that the problem was mine as much as his, I simply returned the book reports marked "no credit," and he left my classroom at the end of the year neither better nor worse because of his exposure to my course.

Guidance personnel are aware of personality clashes, and shift students around when they feel that is the basis of a problem, oftentimes without consulting the teacher. Although personality clashes are harmful when they run rampant, they are not as common as students think. To prevent them an important control factor, public opinion, operates subtly and effectively within the classroom. Most adolescents have a strong sense of justice, and if a teacher heckles a student over a period of time, the teacher is likely to have difficulty with the entire class. Evidence of this was a role-playing incident done in one of my classes one year:

> A group of students enacted a scene from one of their classes in which a teacher had accused a student of lying about a book report that the student claimed she had turned in to the teacher. The students managed to convey in the skit an unpleasant emotional passage in which the teacher had been unfairly hard on the student, and at the conclusion of the skit, the student had run from the room in tears. The question the skit posed was, "What should we do about it?" No one in the class suggested as a possible solution that they should forget it because it was none of their business.

Most of the time when students feel a teacher is picking on them, in truth the teacher is trying to improve undesirable patterns of behavior. One of the important functions of public education is to help our youngsters learn to deal with people they don't naturally deal with well. The teacher frequently becomes the object of this process. One of my students illustrated this quite well:

> Janice Smith disliked her Problems of Democracy teacher so intensely that she was unable to do satisfactory work in the class. When her distress began to affect her other classes as well, she asked me for advice.
>
> I suggested she try a little psychological experiment. "Use a special sheet in your notebook," I said. "Each day when you go to P.O.D. class, write down one thing that you like about the class. Be sure it is genuine. At first it will be hard to find anything, but if you look you can find something. Perhaps it will be the shade of dress that someone is wearing or the way someone smiles when he greets someone across the room. Try hard to find something you like about

the teacher as soon as you can. Then, each day before you go to class, open your notebook to the page you have reserved for this experiment and read it over."

She came down to me the next time she got her report card. "I wanted to tell you that I realized something very important," she said. "It happened before I got my grades. I realized that the grade on my card in P.O.D. doesn't matter. My attitude and my work have improved, and that is what is important." Her grade had not improved at that point, but it did by the end of the year. An easier solution would have been for Janice to change classes, but she gained, by making this experiment, skill in human relations as well as a deeper understanding of what education involved.

Far more prevalent and therefore more devastating than personality clashes in teacher-student relationships is the tendency of teachers to pigeonhole students. The more experienced a teacher is, the more likely he is to do this because the ruts go deeper each time they are used.

I used to think all students who didn't do homework were "bums," i.e., stupid, lazy, dishonest, and likely to be sexually immoral. When looking for an example of prejudice in my own experience to help my students see how to find some of their own, I realized for the first time that some students who don't do homework are creative, powerful individuals who refuse to conform to a system that is wrong for them.

Another example of pigeonholing is when an experienced teacher proudly claims he can predict what his students will make on a test. Such teachers categorize students early in the school year and then hold them in the mold the rest of the time. When students *do* try to improve and work hard to make some progress, they give up and quit if a teacher, so to speak, puts a grade on the test before it is taken.

As one sits in the teacher's room and hears teachers discuss students, the prevalence of this categorizing is quite evident. Teachers swap stories of what to expect from "that type" and impart gems of wisdom about what to do with "such creatures." One wonders what kind of impact this stereotyping is having on young teachers. Perhaps a handbook for beginning teachers should contain a line, "Always put cotton in your ears before entering the teacher's lounge."

Teachers sometimes categorize the good students also, and once a student has made a good impression, he can coast for the rest of the year. Some students try to get good grades by being nice to the teacher. This sickens other students, and the fear of being suspected of "nosing," as the students label it, deters some students from developing any personal relationship with the teacher at all. A clear-cut, objective grading policy which a teacher follows regardless of any personal relationship to the student helps avoid these problems. If, however, a teacher allows a student to come to class late without the required admission slip, the objectivity fades and the student becomes a "teacher's pet."

The prevalence of this tendency to categorize students has an important influence on the entire educational system. It often makes the school more a factory for manufacturing patterns of people than a garden for the growth of individuals. People behave the way they are expected to behave most of the time, and this is especially true in the teacher-student relationship. We teachers too often press students into molds that were shaped by students we taught before, and we hold them there. If at first a student doesn't fit the mold in which we place him, he frequently changes his behavior to fit the pattern we expect by the end of the year.

PAWING

Sometimes the pawing strikes a spark. Crushes on teachers are fairly common, and occasionally these crushes surface. Two illustrations follow:

Nancy was a quiet student who worried about grades, about getting along with her group, and about life in general. In a vocational conference with her in January, I assured her she was fully capable of succeeding in nurse's training, her field of interest, according to both guidance-test scores and my observance of her performance. I also told her that her overconcern about grades might be producing tension which interfered with her ability to achieve them. After that, she often stopped by my desk just long enough to get a question answered. Then, as the school year was drawing to a close, she made an appointment for a conference after school.

She reminded me of the conference twice before the day arrived, and when she came for it, she was pale and trembling. I thought she must be having some terrible experience of some kind, and waited for her to approach it, but she never did. We talked about her admission to nursing school, which she had arranged since our last interview. She stayed about an hour, during which time I was expecting something important to enter the discussion. At the end of the hour she thanked me and left. After thinking it over, I decided she had just wanted to be with me. I recalled an experience from my youth when I had felt that way about a camp counselor and decided that she had gotten what she wanted from the interview.

Helene revealed a much more serious involvement in her Philosophy of Life paper. She had a crush on her junior high biology teacher, which had so involved her that her schoolwork suffered. When the guidance counselor summoned her for consultation, she confessed her problem. The counselor, well-meaning of course, told her it was wrong to love a married man and used some Bible quotations to prove it.

Her feelings of guilt after this experience finally resulted in psychiatric care, which hadn't helped much because she didn't tell her psychiatrist about her crush. The discussion of crushes in our class gave her a new perspective on her experience, and she freely described it in her paper for me. The six-year interval had taken its toll, however, and her self-confidence was seriously undermined. Although brilliant, she was afraid to try college. At my persuasion, she enrolled, but I do not know if she succeeded.

Teachers have little opportunity to get to know individual students in the classroom. Because I constantly used personal illustrations when I taught, the students learned much about me, but they were not so willing to publicize their personal lives when they recited, and I learned much less about them from this interplay. I did, however, learn much about my students by observing their behavior in the classroom. The way they dress, their attention or lack of attention during class, their behavior with other students fall into a nebulous pattern which gradually takes the shape of a personality.

When students have specific problems, they often approach a teacher individually during the class breaks, but otherwise they stay away from the teacher's desk to avoid a "teacher's pet" label. As the year progresses, especially with seniors, informal interplay of this sort comes more naturally, and by the last month of school a few students may stop by regularly.

Although the time before and after school gives teachers and students opportunities to get acquainted, the students seldom come in. I got to know my homeroom students because we were in the room together before school each morning, but I didn't teach them. Bulletin-board projects often brought students to my classroom before and after school, but students seldom dropped by otherwise unless they had a specific need.

One of the most important avenues of communication I had with students was the papers they wrote for me. In my course, particularly, these papers often revealed important personality qualities. By writing comments on their papers, I made this communication two-way, and by the end of the year, when our work reached its climax with a Philosophy of Life paper, most students had developed enough confidence in me to share important elements in their lives through this paper.

The natural history of how a close relationship developed in class may best clarify the process involved:

The second seat from the right on the back row will always belong to Joe in my classroom. He sat there most of the first quarter unnoticed because he was one of the quiet ones. He had a record of straight Ds in high school, which in his case, put him squarely in the bracket of a psychological dropout. A student needs skill to walk the tight rope that consistently, to be able to judge with that much accuracy the exact minimum each teacher will extract before the D becomes an E. One cannot allow too much margin in what one does because the possibility that the D will become a C is a threat of humiliation too great to bear. Joe had a perfect record when he entered my class.

The first time I noticed him was during a game. Because he took psychology sixth period, on the days we had athletic events he remained in my classroom during the game if he did not purchase a ticket. I usually required students remaining in my classroom to study during that hour so that I could do some of the things always awaiting attention in a classroom. On this particular day, I was trying to put up a bulletin board and asked if anyone in the class could do lettering. When Joe said he could, I was skeptical because I was particular about my lettering, and he didn't look very efficient. I reluctantly supplied him with the materials and the slogan I wanted done, and he worked the rest of the hour on it. When I examined his work, it was with mixed pleasure. He had done a fine job, but he used an ornate English style which no one else could finish. I thanked him anyway and expressed approval of his skill. When the bell rang, he tore out without making any arrangements to finish. The next day I had him complete the work during classtime, and the class managed without him just fine.

Because of this incident, I became aware of Joe and, during a subsequent game, noticed a drawing he was doing, which was a grotesque human figure that clamored for symbolic interpretation.

I told him it struck me as especially interesting to a psychology teacher, and he said he drew a lot because it was an outlet for his emotions.

Then Joe began to buy tickets for the games, and since he remained quiet in class, I forgot he was there until one day I found one of his drawings penciled on the surface of his desk. The author of this work was so distinctly Joe that I could clearly place the blame, and when the class assembled the next day, I gave him an eraser and told him to get to work after a serious sermon about destroying property.

Sometime in November when he was too broke to go to the game, I tried to get him to help tabulate data, but he was suddenly busy with a drawing he was making for world history. He showed me the picture, which was in two sections. Two knights were fighting at the top, and he planned to picture their armor lying around with the knights dissolved at the bottom. As I looked at this drawing, I realized I had never taught a more creative student. I left him to his drawing deeply impressed.

Shortly before Christmas, Joe came up to my desk before class with a full book of typing paper. He handed it to me closed and said, "My Christmas picture is in there."

I opened it to discover a most unusual drawing of a grotesque Santa Claus. After commenting on its cleverness, I passed it around for the class to see. It created so much commotion that I recalled it to explain some of the subtle points: e.g., the barber's pole represented the North Pole, and one of the reindeer flying through the air was a can of Comet cleanser. I did not, however, note the pack filled with skeleton bones since I felt that was self-explanatory.

The day before Christmas vacation I was eating lunch with his art teacher. She was young, charming, warm and a conventional sort of person. "Nice" is the word to describe her. She was complaining because the other students in her accelerated art class were imitating Joe's drawings. She then went on to describe a picture of Joe's which she had taken home and hung in her bedroom. The drawing contained a peaked mountain with a long, winding trail leading to an outhouse perched on top of the mountain. Stretched along the trail lay a skeleton, reaching for the top. Although amused by this drawing, the art teacher was also a little embarrassed and had relegated it to the bedroom. For the first time, I began to wonder about Joe. From what could such sophistication arise with a background like his? He worked at a hamburger joint nights to pay his board and room and buy his own clothes because his family was so poor.

That same day, Joe swept into class white and tense.

"Do you think I am a sadist?" he demanded.

"Not by a long shot," I replied without hesitation.

"Miss Downing says I am!" he said. This was his history teacher, a highly respected member of our staff who had been teaching many years.

Joe was quiet for a moment. Then he added, "I got a failure notice."

"Perhaps she was trying to improve your study habits," I suggested.

"Well, they could be improved," he admitted, "but I like Miss Downing." He turned dejectedly to his seat, and I went on with the class.

I couldn't get Joe out of my mind during the holidays. I was more upset about the teacher than anything else because although some teachers fling psychological terms around for effect without knowing what they mean, she was not one of them. I was sure she meant what she said to Joe, and so was he. When school reconvened after the holidays, I asked Joe to see me at his convenience. When he came up after class, I told him that although I was not capable of judging or interpreting his drawings, I was certain they were not sadistic. "They reflect a society in turmoil," I said, "but they are humorous and idealistic rather than sadistic." He thanked me and went on to catch his bus.

The next morning I went to see his art teacher who knew also about the sadistic accusation and realized it had disturbed Joe. I expressed the opinion that Joe should be allowed to develop in his own way and that he needed to be let alone. Even though she agreed, the grotesque figures faded from Joe's drawings after that.

Joe and I, however, had discovered some common sparks in our personalities, and our relationship grew rapidly. Coming to psychology from art, he developed the habit of bringing his drawings to me before class. I would hang them on the board and wait for students to ask what they meant, which the students always did. They were fascinated by his work, and the drawings were so loaded with meaning that they often made a good psychology lesson. One picture I remember had rows of manhole covers indicating that society was living underground. The students' responses to this work lit a fire in Joe's life. Sophisticated as he was, he too needed a place among his fellow students, and he had a solid one in psychology class.

I saw very little of Joe outside of class. His bus came early, and he used to meet me in the hall to say, "Good morning," but that was all he said. Once or twice, when he faced a crisis such as a breakup with his girl friend or a family row, he came down to my room before school to tell me. We had little communication through his papers because he continued his twelve-year program of doing no homework for school. He always took tests, however, and almost always passed them. One test he failed, he covered with drawings illustrating the reasons why he had failed.

Seeing Joe in the library one day, I teased him a little about doing his personality analysis, a long-term assignment I knew he would not do for me. Suddenly serious, I asked, "Whom would you like to do?"

"I thought I might do Dali," he replied.

I left him thinking, "Of course, he should do an artist and a modern one at that."

That afternoon he strode into my room, slammed a book on my desk, and shouted, "Look at that!"

He had reason for his excitement. Contained in the book were some pen-and-ink drawings by Dali, which were so much like Joe's that they could easily have been his. The same grotesque human figures, the same kind of line, the same kind of symbolic effect that I had made Joe erase from the top of his desk earlier in the year were weirdly there in that book.

Class interrupted our excited perusal, but after class Joe came up and said, "I don't know if I'm glad or sorry. I'm glad because it means my drawings are good, but I am sorry because someone else has already created what I thought I had done."

"Are you sure you've never seen them?" I asked.

"Positive," he said. "All I've ever seen have been paintings."

By then, Joe had taken to storing his artwork behind the filing cabinet in my room because he had no place at home to keep it. Although I had no doubt of the value of his pen-and-ink sketches because they were so exciting to me, I was not so sure about the talent in his paintings. With his permission, I took them to two artists I knew who were qualified to judge their merits, and they both felt his work showed unusual talent and promise.

He presented me with my portrait (I was a prancing white stallion), which he included in his one-man art show in the school library. This show created so much excitement among the students that Joe himself became convinced that he was talented.

In a talk with Joe about his vocational interests, I tried to encourage him to pursue art training after high school. He had planned to join the Navy after he graduated and take pharmacist's training. Although he had ample intelligence, his orientation toward school precluded college. I tried to encourage him to investigate various kinds of art training available in the community and let him alone otherwise.

I hated to see Joe move into his uneasy world when he was about to graduate. The school had done something important for him in helping him realize that he had not only ability but also talent, but was this enough? I gave him some art materials—paper and pen and ink—after commencement, feeling that such a gift might symbolize the importance of what he had learned about himself in school. Giving him the package, I said, "When you are famous, my portrait will be worth a fortune, but I won't sell it!"

As he grinned and thanked me for the gift, we shook hands and said good-bye.

Joe has kept in touch with me since graduation. We both thought he was going to succeed at first when he became an apprentice to a lithographer. It seemed ideal, but for some reason he blew up and quit the job after about eighteen months. He worked nights in a food store long enough to complete barbering school. Now he has joined the Navy and is cutting hair for sailors. Although barbering is an art of sorts, one must admit he is tamed.

Most of the personal interaction between teachers and students is casual and relaxed, providing a richness to the school day. John looked like a movie star and acted like the strong, silent type. My day always picked up when he came by to give his pleasant greeting. Adele, too intelligent to spend much time in close attention to the slow pace of the class, reported her progress with her boy friend after class because this was not so easy for her. Gregory, poised and self-assured, took an easy place with a group of girls not of his social class because I asked his aid to even the groups.

In a high school student's search for identity, he begins seriously to ask questions about himself. "What am I like?" "How do I seem to other people?" "What are my strengths and weaknesses?" He finds important mirrors in his teachers. His parents love him too much to be an objective reflection. Whether they are too permissive, too demanding, or somewhere in-between, they make too blurred an image for him to get an objective view of himself. In his teachers, however, he finds a judgment based on what he is. A teacher may grow to love him, too, but here this is an earned love based on his personality and his ability to relate deeply to someone who doesn't have to love him. Teachers also do much to help a student find his ability level and decide what he should expect from himself effectively. Grades help here, in spite of their hazards, and in classwork he finds areas of endeavor that are of interest to him so that he can look somewhat more objectively toward vocational choices.

Whether the pawing is clawing or petting, personal relations between teachers and students are the basis of much that is important in the service education renders society. Behavior change travels across a bridge of emotion, and it is from person to person that the most important changes occur. This taming goes deep.

CHAPTER SEVEN

They Stretch

RELATIONSHIPS BETWEEN STUDENTS

"But, in essence, the classroom is more than just a fact-compiling center; it is, in fact, the one place where friends can see and work with each other five days a week for at least an hour each day," writes Geraldine Motts, a senior.

A student theme for English class describes a classroom as follows:

> A student sees quite a few things going on in geometry
> class that a teacher sitting up front does not see.
> I see Gene crouching behind Pat while writing a
> letter to his girl. Larry and his neighbor are too
> engulfed in their tic-tac-toe game to notice Mark who
> has just stuck his compass in his finger while showing
> off to Bonnie. Jane is frantically trying to finish or copy
> her homework while Doug is waiting impatiently to
> retrieve his notes from her. Sam has just successfully
> launched a paper airplane and is grinning with delight
> as it floats around the room leaving a path of distracted
> students in its flight. Meanwhile a trio up front is
> laughing at each other's jokes while Edith sits in her
> seat looking utterly disgusted.

Much of value occurs in such a situation although little of it is accumulation of subject matter. Gene and Mark are developing courting techniques, a skill highly needed by today's adolescents. Larry and his neighbor are improving their social relationships, and Jane and Doug are cooperating, another necessary talent in today's complex society. Sam has developed a sensitivity to people's responses and is learning how to manipulate them. And who in our society today can deny the importance of skill at telling jokes? The light touch at the crucial moment can save a peace talk or swing a contract. Edith seems to be the only loser at the moment.

THE COMMON VIEW

Interactions between students lay groundwork for most behavior changes. Students can learn far more from each other than they can learn from adults because they function from a similar frame of reference. This frame of reference means primarily a point of view. Three basic reasons may help account for the power of peer-group relations during adolescence. One of the effects of our vast educational program in this country has been to segregate children by age levels throughout their developing years. This is different from the family-centered culture of our rural society in which one's relationships consisted mainly of associating with brothers and sisters of varying ages. Even the rural one-room school house combined all age groups. Today, the segregation of age groups in the school has spread to the neighborhood, the church, and even club activities for children. This means that youngsters function mainly in a social medium of others who are at the same stage of development as they are. The similar stage of development contributes to a common frame of reference.

A second factor which makes the peer group so important to adolescents is the fact that they live in an amalgamated culture. The adolescent peer group serves as a vital link between the value system of a student's own family, which may vary greatly from one family to another, and his adult value system, which must serve him in his contacts with the many varieties of values he meets in his adult life. On the basis of the security derived from the age group, which shares many common views, he can recognize that differences in values exist without being shattered by them. An adolescent, for example, coming from a home where drinking is a sin, may find classmates he admires who have a different view of drinking. He may or may not retain his own family's value, but regardless of his position on drinking he is able to relate to the other student in regard to taste in music, the right thing to wear, and enthusiasm for the school's football hero, and in this medium he is able to develop a sophisticated tolerance for the difference.

Most important of all, the adolescent peer group serves as the hub of the wheel of social change. Because adult values do not always apply to the world as it has become, youth have developed a value system of their own which gives sustenance to the members who create it. United they can face the world and sustain each other. In this manner, they do not go off on dangerous tangents alone. Quite to the contrary, the teen-age value system is quite rigid in itself, but it does serve as a stabilizing influence during this period of change even while it allows for the progression of values in the wider society.

In the medium of the adolescent peer group, the modern teenager finds his identity—an honest, objective view of what he is—reflected from the behavior of others who understand him. Much of the interaction upon which this is based occurs within the classroom.

THE PROCESS

The poet Gibran has said, "No man can reveal to you aught but that which lies half asleep in the dawning of your knowledge." In any group of students there are some who are a little ahead of the others, and they can point the way far more effectively than adults who function from a much different frame of reference. The classroom serves as a laboratory for these relationships whether the teacher plans it, is merely aware of it, or is ignorant of it.

A dramatic illustration of this occurred in my classroom once:

A student went into a trance right in my classroom. She came in and sat down, but when her friends tried to talk to her, she did not respond. When they told me, I went over to her, called her by name, and touched her, but she continued to stare straight ahead with a glazed expression in her eyes. Realizing her condition was serious, I sent for the nurse, who was also unable to rouse Ruth and was as much at a loss to know how to deal with the situation as I was. Believing her condition to be an emotional upheaval, I ran to the office and called a psychiatrist I knew for directions. He said to get her out of the classroom and contact her parents about hospitalization.

By the time I returned to the classroom, the nurse had talked to Ruth's mother, who claimed the child was "just acting." We sent for the stretcher, and some of the boys from my class carried her to the infirmary. The principal, learning of the emergency, called an ambulance which took her to the hospital. As we were starting a unit on mental health that day in class, I talked frankly to the class about Ruth. I said that her problems were probably primarily emotional, that she was likely to be out for a while, and that when she came back, it would be very important to her how we treated her.

When Ruth came back to school after several weeks of absence, I felt her chances of graduating were slim. Nothing had changed in her family situation to ease the stress that had precipitated her breakdown. Her mother was in the late stages of a menopause pregnancy and blamed psychology for all Ruth's difficulties. She believed that Ruth, who was an avid reader, read about weird patterns of behavior and then acted them out. Her father was trying to make a living for his family by some kind of unsatisfactory night job. One brother, a year older than Ruth, was flunking senior English for the second time and would not graduate. A younger brother, whom Ruth dearly loved, often took the brunt of the frustrations of his unhappy parents, and this was the hardest of all for Ruth to bear. An aunt had taken care of Ruth when she was first released from the hospital, but she was now home again.

The class was glad to see her back. They made her welcome, but maintained a delicacy of concern that showed great skill in

human relations. No one shunned her, but neither did they overwhelm her with attention.

The crucial incident that occurred came up most unexpectedly. We were initiating our group projects on role playing. Since this was a new activity for the students, I was attempting to demonstrate the process so that each group would have some idea of how to go about developing its own presentation. I asked for someone to volunteer to describe some problem that was bothering them.

Ruth volunteered. As she was quick with ideas and outgoing, this was common practice with her. The problem she suggested dealt with a book she had taken from the revolving paperback library we maintained in psychology class. The book, *Jordi,* by Theodore Isaac Rubin, contained two psychoanalytic case studies. When Ruth's mother found the book, she had commandeered it so that Ruth was unable to return the book to the library. Her question was, "What should I do?"

The scene which we decided to act was between Ruth and her mother with Ruth playing her own role and another student playing her mother. They acted out the discovery of the book and the fight that followed. When the fight reached a sufficient pitch to get everyone involved, I interrupted the drama and opened the class discussion with the question, "Do any of you have any suggestions about how Ruth could deal with her problem?"

A few tentative suggestions were made. Then Jane stood up and took a step or two toward Ruth, who was still standing from the play.

"Ruth, have you ever told your mother that you *loved* her?" she asked.

A loud silence filled the room. In that silence, students changed. Ruth was aware for the first time in all her troubles that part of the difficulty lay within herself. Of course she hadn't told her mother that she loved her. She didn't love her. But suddenly she saw that Jane loved her mother, that such a relationship was possible, and that it was something worth striving for.

As the only child of a wealthy family, Jane had been protected, coddled, and loved. Her father was struggling to overcome a serious health problem, and she had suffered so with her concern over him that she had a serious health problem herself. At this moment, though, she knew she loved her mother *and* her father, and whatever their problems were, there was a good basis for coping with them because of this love.

I believe that every student in the class felt something important about their relationships with their parents too. They were at an age when these are difficult and when the giving of love to their parents instead of receiving it is a giant step forward into maturity.

We found an easy solution to Ruth's immediate problem of the book by suggesting that she pay the twenty-five-cent fine required for unreturned books and let her mother keep the book. Her long-term problem, that of her relationship to her mother, we could not solve, but I do believe that this experience gave her new direction. At least she was able to maintain enough stability for the remainder of the year to graduate.

SILENT CONTROLS

The strongest control in the classroom is the fear that students have that their fellow students will disapprove of what they are doing. The two examples which follow give evidence of this:

Early in my teaching career when I was struggling with discipline problems, I had one class that I couldn't control. It was composed mostly of boys, and Pete did far more than the others to keep things stirred up. I could never pin down his actions enough to send him out for discipline because he was clever enough to disguise his activity. One day when I had given up doing anything constructive with general activity for the class because of their misbehavior, I was trying to put some study questions on the board so that I could put them to writing. While my back was turned, a low whistle started in the class. Such an activity is impossible to locate, and the students were waiting with great amusement to see what I would do about it. In desperation, I sent Pete to the office with a note saying he was whistling in my class. This action worked beautifully as far as the class was concerned. They settled down because I had done something about my problem, and they respected me for it.

However, the vice-principal never forgave me. Our conversation went something like this:

VP: "Pete says he wasn't whistling."

Me: "I don't know if it was Pete or not."

VP: "Then why did you send him down?"

Me: "He is the one in the class who most deserves to be punished, and I had to do something to stop the whistling."

VP: "I don't understand you."

My mistake, of course, was in trying to get the vice-principal to understand the dynamics of the class. I should have just said, "Do you believe me or Pete?" The class understood that justice was being done, and Pete would have accepted their judgment.

The importance of public opinion in the classroom was brought forcibly to my attention one year when I was berating one of my classes for their lack of questioning.

"Why don't you raise more questions?" I asked.

"Teachers don't want us to ask questions," one student replied.

"They don't always know the answers, and they don't want to admit it so they discourage questions."

"Look what happened to me," another contributed. "I raised my hand in English class and asked a simple question. The teacher told me to look it up. I'm a conscientious student so I did. When I brought the answer in, the teacher said, 'That's fine. Now write a paper on it.' So here I am, stuck with writing a paper just because I asked an innocent question in class."

"Teachers make fun of us when we ask questions," a third said.

This sounded provocative to me, and so I discussed it at the lunch table with some fellow teachers. I had never stopped to analyze how I handled student questions, and this factor seemed rather important to me now. I admitted to the others that I sometimes hesitated to give direct answers to student's questions because I thought some discussion of them would engender more thought than a direct answer. The other teachers seemed to feel confident that they handled student questions with competence. I was interested in the discrepancy between the point of view of teachers and students.

"Let's make a survey," I suggested to the class when we gathered after lunch. They agreed, so we set up a form sheet. This form sheet had a place for the question asked and a check line for each of the following responses:

I. Teacher answered.
II. Class discussed.
III. Look it up.
IV. Ignored.
V. Ridiculed.
VI. Answered by a student.
VII. Otherwise handled.

The class was instructed to keep a record in all their classes of questions asked and check the type of response given for one week. The students arranged among themselves to avoid duplication. The results were as follows:

RESPONSES

	I.	II.	III.	IV.	V.	VI.	VII.
Number	123	36	12	6	5	6	0
Percent	65	19	6	3	3	3	

Assuming that categories III, IV, and V, totaling 12 percent, are likely to discourage student questions, we concluded that this alone could scarcely account for the few questions that high school seniors raise.

We decided after some discussion that the answer lies more clearly in the attitudes of the students in the classroom. Most of all, the student is afraid his question may sound dumb, not to the teacher as much as to his fellow students. Second, his question may force his fellow students to listen to a boring harange from the teacher that they don't want to hear. Third, there is always the danger that asking questions might be too eager beaverish, and the other students might suspect him of trying to influence the teacher. All in all, students feel safer if they limit questions to those regarding tests or homework.

Sometimes this public-opinion force present in the classroom gets out of hand. An example occurred in one of my classes one hot spring day:

> I had a feeling of some undercurrent in the classroom, which I could not identify. Whatever was happening involved interaction among the students, but I could not find the source of the excitement.
>
> We paused during the lunch-hour shift because of noise in the halls, and I took this opportunity to write some study questions on the board. The undercurrent grew while my back was turned. I resented the necessity for the interruption and didn't much care how the students wasted the interval while we were waiting for the hall noise to subside. The usual conversation hum was punctuated with giggles. Although curious about what was causing this action, I was not alarmed about it and continued my task at the board.
>
> When the halls quieted down, I turned back to settle the class. They acquiesced with reasonable admonitions, although the process took a little time. As I proceeded with the lesson, I realized that whatever had started before the interlude had picked up momentum. By now the giggles had turned to bursts of laughter. As the students realized I was seeking the source of the interplay, a game developed which we played until the end of the hour. When the bell rang, I went back to my corner defeated. As the class drifted out I asked a couple of students near my desk what had been going on.
>
> "Jim was mimicking Terry," one replied.
>
> The next thing I knew Terry was in trouble with the office for fighting. Jim, carried away with the exultation of leading the class in this exciting adventure, had accosted Terry in the hall outside my door after class and picked a fight with him.
>
> Terry was a scapegoat. The reasons for this were never clear to me except he didn't like to fight. He was over six feet tall and well

built, although no muscleman. He had close-cropped, kinky-curly blond hair and blue eyes, wore thick glasses, and had some acne. Although he lacked the polished look that many adolescents achieve, he was reasonably neat and clean. He came from the poorest home in the poorest section of town, but he was intelligent and worked fairly hard on his schoolwork and very hard at making friends. No one dared to be his friend because Terry did not want to fight. The boys at the bus stop made his life miserable. They teased him, pushed him around, and even beat up on him, but he would not fight back. His reputation as a sissy followed him to school, and whatever he did, kids made fun of him and laughed at him.

Jim was a skipper. His irregular attendance in school had interfered seriously with his achievement, and he was failing my course. When I asked him to come in after school to discuss this problem, he had told me about his family situation. His parents had recently been divorced, and he was living in a boarding house with his mother. They did not get along at all well, and he wanted to leave her but had no place to go.

The class had been killing a dead hour with a touch of humor, little realizing the potency of their collective power, but it is always there.

The tone of this public opinion can change rapidly. In one of the role-playing incidents acted out in my class one year, a group of students depicted a scene in another teacher's class where this happened:

> The teacher was having serious difficulty with discipline problems in general, and on this particular day, when he turned his back to the class to write on the board, one or two of the boys started throwing pieces of chalk and wads of paper at the teacher. The class was enjoying this and encouraged the action by laughing at it. The teacher turned on the class furiously and assigned them all a two-hundred word essay. The problem my students were concerned with in the skit was, "What should we do to avoid this group punishment when only two students were responsible?" The boys who precipitated the crisis had changed from heroes to heels.

From these examples of group processes occurring in the classroom, one sees that the opinion of the class as a whole is a constant shaping force in the personality development of the student. Each student carefully culls his behavior, eliminating patterns that bring rejection from his fellow students and replaying those patterns that bring approval and acceptance. Furthermore, he becomes aware of the common experiences he shares with others in the group and borrows some of the solutions of others that fit his needs. In this kind of stretching, the taming has power.

<h3 align="center">INTERPLAY</h3>

Fully as important as these attitudes in behavior change are the personal relationships which develop between individuals in classroom activity. A student writes, "Besides learning, the classroom is a place where students get together and develop their social connections. They make friends and further their knowledge by relating past experiences with each other."

> I once taught a class composed entirely of boys, none of whom could be classed as scholars. At times in that class important knowledge was gained, but by spring the students were badly out of control. We took stock one day of the reasons why, and I listed them on the board:
> "We have no girls to put us on our good behavior."
> "It is spring and we get antsy in the spring."
> "It's all your fault. You *made* us get acquainted, and now we know each other so well that we can't be formal with each other."
> The list was too formidable so I put them to writing for the rest of the year. We had already accomplished much in that class, and I was content.

The classroom is an important medium for these relationships for several reasons. In the first place, the classroom is a meeting ground for the youngsters. Even students who hate school tire of vacations before they are over because of the need for the associations that occur in the classroom and within the school situation in general. Those who like school enjoy it more because of these opportunities to associate with other students their age than because of a deep thirst for knowledge. My psychological dropouts were never loners. No one seemed able to get as far as eleventh or twelfth grade without either social or academic satisfaction in school.

The classroom is more than just a meeting place, however. It is structured in relation to the activity that occurs there. Small-group discussions are difficult to do well because so many groups lose direction after the first few moments. The students revert to personal chatter and sense even more than the teacher that such activity is a waste of time. Even the personal chatter becomes desultory. This is in marked contrast to the buzz of conversation that bubbles up during a lull in classroom activity. The interplay during lulls has vitality because the students know it isn't going to last very long. Another example of how important the structure of the classroom activity is is the deadliness of students confined to the classroom during game time. Students purchasing tickets are excused, and if only a few remain, many teachers allow the students to socialize during that hour. An hour is a long time to kill with sparkling conversation when there is nothing going on to stimulate it, and at this time the interpersonal relationships are sluggish to say the least.

Also the structure of classroom activity provides a groundwork for the development of interpersonal relationships. If the student is bored with what is going on, interplay with another student creates a diversion from the boredom. If the student is angry about what is going on, he can release some of the steam by showing it to his neighbor. If the student is excited about what is going on, he wants to share this excitement with those around him. A constant undercurrent of interaction between students provides steady nourishment for the process of becoming.

The classroom is an important medium for this teen-age development also because it is controlled and directed by the teacher. About the second quarter of the term, after I had oriented my classes toward some degree of self-direction, I moved my desk to the back of the room. I didn't always stay there because I had to go to the front to conduct discussions or lecture or give directions. However, I worked hard at making my classes student-centered rather than teacher-centered, and much of the time I was back at my desk while the students took over. This was good when it happened, but it was not easily achieved nor could it go along indefinitely without me. Any group of youngsters, even seniors in high school, needs the balance of mature judgment, and the classroom has this. Sometimes it has *only* direction, but too much of it is better than none at all.

Another reason why the classroom is such an important medium is its continuity. The students see each other an hour a day each school day for 180 days. With the volatile nature of friendships at this age, this continuity is important. Students keep on seeing their friends in class whether they are up or down in their relationships with them.

A romance developed in one of my classes last year between a Jewish girl and a boy from a rigid Presbyterian family. He was shy and inhibited, but a surprisingly deep thinker, and she was warm, alive, and open about all her feelings. They were good for each other, and the romance spread some of its sparkle around the class. After a fairly serious discussion about religious differences in marriage in class one day, I noticed that Lois was hating school and flouncing around class with a fury born of rejection. Ed had stopped dating her, I presume because he decided he was getting too serious, but they still had to see each other in class every day. This romance had gone deep, but by the end of the year they had developed at least a surface sophistication in their relationship. The necessity of seeing each other in class resulted in thickening the skin of what would have otherwise been a tender relationship.

This undercurrent of action is continuous, even in a formal class. One year a student gave me a blow-by-blow description of her developing romance in the class she had the period before mine. Some days it was just the way the boy looked at her that she reported, and one day when things weren't going so well, the fact that he *hadn't* looked at her was what mattered. Students are constantly aware of what others are doing, and much of their communication comes from observation of behavior cues.

Of course, another source of communication is talking, which they do every chance they get. This varies greatly with the formality of the classroom atmosphere, but some occurs in even the most formal of classes before and after the bell. An informal atmosphere gives frequent opportunities for personal interchange, and on some occasions when a class discussion gets hot, a bursting out of chatter between students indicates interest they must share with each other.

A third method of communication in the classroom is notewriting. Most of this is done by girls, although a boy in love will also indulge. I know much of this goes on, but I have little conception of the contents. Once in awhile a teacher commandeered a note that livened up the teacher's room, but I never read the few I found in my classes. Actually, I seldom saw them, because the students are careful about keeping them under cover. Evidence of their frequency can be found in any room after school, however, by observing the tiny bits of paper stuffed under the desks. Students are careful to tear up their personal notes completely so they cannot be reconstructed. Other evidence comes from student conversations, which frequently refer to notewriting as an important classroom pastime.

This undercurrent of action sometimes bubbles to the surface when support is needed. One technique I have used to utilize this potential is to state, "We will have a quiz if there is enough time after your questions about the material it will cover are answered." Usually the class rallied with enough questions to fill the hour, and I enjoyed watching them work at it. Under these circumstances, the hero is the one who can think of the most questions, regardless of their merit.

Sometimes this undercurrent shows up as cheating. Students' attitudes toward each other's schoolwork give some evidence to support the idea that we may be moving from a competitive to a cooperative society.

Geraldine writes:

> Since the classroom is composed of friends, the teacher can expect at least a little sign of loyalty among the students—sticking together against the teacher, helping each other during tests and doing their classwork and homework together. The teacher, therefore, is fighting a losing battle against the one true trait of friendship, which is loyalty to each other no matter what the risk.

Of course they copy homework. They think it's just something the teacher thought up to keep them busy anyway, and they wouldn't think of refusing it to a friend when asked. Copying on tests is about the same. If a student is trying to look at another student's paper, most students will move over so his friend can see it without attracting the teacher's attention. In the next breath they may criticize violently the student across the room who is doing the same thing, however. Although they tend to pay lip service to the principle of this kind of honesty, in practice they cooperate. They are more concerned about their fellow student's opinion of them than they are about getting a better grade than he.

Cribbing, i.e., bringing to class material that contains correct

Information and using it during the exam, is a much more serious offense according to their value system, and surprisingly little of that goes on in high school. If a teacher stalks the room during an exam, students tend to crib more than if the teacher makes it clear to the class that honesty is important, but the only way it can be achieved is for the students to demand it from themselves. Too close a watch seems to challenge the students to a contest, and some crib who wouldn't think of doing so otherwise. If a teacher doesn't seem to care one way or another, this also seems to invite cribbing. Students like to think the teacher is responsible for keeping them honest, but they know it isn't true.

When I first started teaching, I made up different exams for each class so that the students would not pass information about the tests from one class to another. I gave this up quite soon because it was much work, it forced weaker exams, and it wasn't necessary. On essay quizzes I changed the questions after lunch because the students passed those questions along while they were eating, but they exchanged very few objective questions. Students talked about how difficult the tests were, and might describe some areas of information covered, but only once in my teaching career did I find an actual copy of a test used. Even in this case, it was only the last page of an eight-page test. Of course, such cheating probably happened more than once, but not often.

Students talk about how prevalent cheating is, but they are somewhat like journalists. Sins make more lively conversation, and I think that although these practices varied from one class to another, students talked more than they acted. Many students have a moral wrestling bout when they see other students cheating (other than the copying which they subconsciously accept). This problem came up quite often in our role-playing incidents, and the solutions suggested were always nebulous. The students were torn between the conflicting values of loyalty and honesty, and usually wound up concluding that half a decision was better than none. They would try to do *something* about the situation, but that something was never to tell on their fellow students.

PERSON TO PERSON

Types of relations in the classroom vary greatly. Friendships (i.e., a relationship based on intellectual and social attractions as contrasted to physical) vary in depth from a casual speaking acquaintance to a friendship deep enough to last a lifetime. By the senior year in high school, most students are firm enough in their ability to relate to the opposite sex that friendship flows freely with either sex, although best friends tend to be of the same sex.

The growth of friendship during the high school years is often a changeable process. During childhood, association between friends tends to be fairly smooth because it is casual. One child is willing to give up some of his selfish interests to accommodate to those of another child because it is more fun to play with him than it is to play alone and have his own way. During adolescence involvement becomes much deeper. One chooses one's friends by this age, and the choice is based on finding someone whose interests and needs complement or supplement his own to such a degree that the relationship itself becomes a need Then he becomes vulnerable. His friends can hurt him, and teen-agers are often hurt. Girls who are best friends one day say nasty things to each other, don't speak, or talk about their former friend behind her back the next day. Boys fight, heckle, or ignore; then they get over being angry and go back to being friends again.

Through my years of teaching, I discovered that the students who were unwilling to labor at the task of building friendships with their age-mates were likely candidates for unhappy lives. Almost every year at least one student was too adult in his attitudes to mingle. Current popular music sounded raucous to him; idealizing facets of school life seemed illogical; the chatter of his fellow students was boring; fads of dress seemed silly. These students were alone in a tragic way, and in their loneliness they struck out ineffectively to ease the condition. One girl fell in love with a married man. Another, who was valedictorian of her class, was so acutely conscious of her lack of ability to relate to the other students that she lacked confidence in her ability to do anything. One boy developed a rich motel life with his first girl friend in spite of a fundamentalist religious faith. Another couldn't make it to school because of a series of illnesses caused by his unhappiness to such a degree that he almost didn't graduate from high school. He scorned college for a business career in a grocery store because he was so alone among his age-mates. One common element in the life history of these students appeared in their Philosophy of Life papers, which they wrote at the end of the year. These students had all been raised in their preschool years in an environment devoid of companionship anywhere near their age. Their companions at this age had been limited to adults.

Of course, we also have romance in the classroom. These are the courtship years, and wherever young people are together, the process simmers. The consistency of the classroom relationship gives a long-term exposure and sees students through the ups and downs in the courtship process that might fall apart under more voluntary conditions. Both boys and girls preen their feathers and strut at every opportunity. Senior boys are under high pressure from the basic physical sex drive. Their sexual power has matured, but they have not yet learned the techniques of control that a more mature man possesses. A wise teacher is cautious about asking a boy to stand when he seems reluctant to do so because he may be concealing an erection. Sex behavior in girls is much more subtle, but it is also much more constant. The eternal hair brushing and lipsticking of a sophomore girl has gone underground to posture poses and gracious gestures in the senior, but to some degree a girl is always trying to be provocative. Many teachers feel that today's short skirts give girls a head start on the game of sex, but I am of the opinion that a sex object is a sex object regardless of how much of it is showing. What a girl does with her exposed legs determines more nearly whether or not the boy across from her can hear the lesson going on in the classroom.

Homosexual attractions occur in the classroom also. These are so far underground that the participants themselves are often unaware of them. I am constantly amazed at the fact that a society as sex-centric as ours recoils in such terror at the thought of homosexuality. The students in my classes discussed without a blush the problem of the new morality and frankly admitted that they didn't see why they shouldn't have sex relations before marriage, but any discussion of homosexuality other than a definition of it or a joke about "queers" would have created serious tension.

I just had fleeting glimpses of homosexual attraction now and then. One was the concern of a girl whose parents weren't letting her see her girl friend, and she was unaware herself of why she cared so much. Another was the light on a boy's face whenever he had an opportunity to refer to or relate to one of the football heroes we had in class. A classroom is a slice of life, and it contains some sampling of all the elements that compose living.

THE HEAD OF THE PARADE

The classroom can also be a training ground for leadership. As a contained and continuous area of interaction, it has all the facilities needed. It even has an enemy—the teacher—and this threat from outside can be a powerful stimulus to the potential leadership contained within the student group. One of the exciting things about teaching is the process of identifying the leaders in the group. This identification process is partly a creative process also because as the leaders become identified, they are created.

In my early years of teaching when I asked the class to elect a secretary, the students often responded by electing the worst male character in the room to serve as my helper. They did this as a joke, of course, but the effect was startling. Not one of these secretaries ever did an inadequate job. The responsibilities of the office often were the only constructive things they did in the classroom, but they always did them well. Furthermore, the class, having put this person in this position, followed his bidding, and he attained stature among his peers.

One of the strongest leaders in any of my classes last year escaped identification by me until the last quarter of the year. The students were way ahead of me on this one. He was a good example of a psychological dropout. He never turned in homework or recited in class, but he came fairly regularly and he consistently passed tests. I should have taken the cue when the group he was in named themselves after him. "Comer's Corner" they called themselves, and I innocently thought they were being facetious. One of the students told me after the year was over that his group used to keep score of how many times I rubbed my nose (one of my nervous habits) during class.

Sometime in March we were going to read a play in class. I had chosen the cast quite carefully because the play needed to be read well to get the meaning across. The day of the performance when the lead male was absent, the class suggested Jules to fill the role. Their unanimity shocked me because I had a low opinion of his ability, but I agreed and he did a good job although a little nervous.

During our Philosophy of Life unit each group was responsible for planning a day's lesson. Comer's Corner was composed of five boys who were above involvement in conventional classroom affairs. I blush to admit that when their period was scheduled I had prepared myself with a substitute lesson in case they did not function.

Jules stood up when I turned the class over to the group and conducted one of the most provocative lessons I have ever attended. Our topic for the week was various philosophical positions regarding immortality. He asked several members of the class who represented various religious faiths to relate their position on this question. The thing that made this lesson powerful was the skill with which he had chosen the speakers. I realized that he had missed nothing in our previous class discussions because he not only picked the ones with the views he wanted represented, but also picked the ones who were temperamentally suited to a genuine sharing with the other students.

He concluded the panel with his own views—an atheist's concept of immortality related to the creative powers of man. He was more advanced in his thinking on philosophical questions than most high school students, and members of the class were shocked at his position. They could hear with understanding what he was saying, however, because he was one of them. His leadership was clarified by this class session, and for the remainder of the year he was the pivot of class action.

How much of this leadership developed during the year and how much was already there from the beginning is unclear, but perhaps not important. Leadership needs to be practiced to stay alive, and the classroom is a fertile ground for either its development or its practice.

Teacher-training courses talk much about using leaders to help further the objectives of the teacher in the classroom. The idea is to get the leaders on your side and let them do your work for you. I always felt that the moment a leader in a class of students undertook my objectives, he became a follower instead of a leader. Leaders in a class may, at times, be trying to please the teacher, but they are doing it their way and not the teacher's if they are truly leaders.

An example of this may clarify my meaning:

My classes worked on various group projects through the year in permanent groups. The most successful of these projects was bulletin-board construction. One group which had proved itself quite outstanding on a previous performance was selected to do a bulletin board which would be up during the evaluation our school was having. The members of the group came to school one night to work on this project, and I went over to let them in.

This group had a leader whose skill was remarkable. On their first bulletin-board performance, I hadn't expected much. The group was composed of two girls and four boys who were all average or below-average students, and when we started to criticize the bulletin board, I was quite shocked to find a highly perceptive theme built subtly into it.

The topic assigned was inferiority complexes. The students developed the title, "How Would You View Yourself if You Were Here?" with a man made of pipe cleaners seated in a wheelchair and looking at himself in a mirror. The subtlety of the wheelchair impressed me because it implied a crutch of sympathy. This I could not believe these youngsters capable of deliberately planning. Deeper meaning slips in accidentally once in awhile, and after looking the group over a little more carefully, I decided no one in the group could possibly have developed it consciously. I continued with the criticism of the bulletin board, trying to get the class to find this theme, which they finally succeeded in doing. "The Whirlwinds," as they called themselves, got their A because they had done an outstanding production, and I kept my doubts about their intentional planning of it to myself.

A few weeks later we were trying some brainstorming in class, a technique used to encourage creative thinking. We had a contest among the groups to see which group could, in a specified amount of time, get the most suggestions of ways to relieve students of carrying so many books. One of the other groups in this class contained most of the good students, and when we tallied the scores, I declared that group the winner. One of the boys in "The Whirlwinds" raised his hand, "How many did you say we got?" he asked. I checked the papers and found they had about twenty more ideas than the group I had declared winners. I apologized for the error and gave them the prize (another A).

I then took a third look at the members of the group, and this time I found him. Bill was a quiet one, often absent. I scarcely knew him by name. He did homework assignments quite regularly, and although they were carelessly done, they did show ability. He made easy Cs in spite of his very poor attendance. I doubt if the rest of the class ever knew he was there, but the members of his group adored him. He made each member feel important, and they gave him everything they had to give on every group project they did all year. He pulled instead of pushed, and one had to look carefully when the group was in action to find the source of the stimulus. He asked instead of told, and he understood each person in the group so well that he knew what to ask each one so they would have an answer.

The night they met to do the bulletin board they were all there full of pep and ideas when I arrived to let them in. They explained their plan to me, all talking at once. I didn't think much of their plan and said so, offering, after a period of discussion, an alternate one. This I don't do on class projects, but we were doing this for a special purpose, and I didn't like their plan. I hadn't given Bill time to work his magic. I left them to go to a meeting, promising to be back to check up on them at its conclusion.

When I returned, they were cleaning up to go home. The bulletin board was finished *their* way, not mine. They all waited tensely for my comments, except Bill. He calmly continued cleaning up, because he really didn't care what I thought of their bulletin board. *He* was their leader, not I.

A classroom is a laboratory of human relations. Students learn some things from books and some things from teachers, but most of all they learn from each other. Whether one likes it or not, the school has taken over much of the responsibility for the socialization process of the individual.

For some reason which I have been unable to fathom, when a student begins to look objectively at himself, he sees his faults first rather than his strengths. High school students, even the successful ones, are all constantly struggling against feelings of inferiority. Only through achievement do they overcome these feelings and gain the self-confidence that is the necessary base of an effective adult life. Through their relationships with each other, teen-agers search for and often find this security.

At times, in today's rapidly changing society, teen-agers seem to live in a moral vacuum and are nothing more than the straw men so poignantly described by T. S. Eliot:

> We are the hollow men
> We are the stuffed men
> Leaning together
> Headpiece filled with straw. Alas!

This is not true and will not be true as long as these youth maintain a value system within their own sphere of influence. They may not buy the value system of the adult world, but they have their own values to which they adhere closely. One may be thankful for the classroom, because here the structure of the teen-age culture is maintained, constrained, and directed. The world's best hope that the values of past generations worth maintaining may persist through the holocaust of change facing today's youth lies in this structure.

As they stretch, they tame themselves creatively.

CHAPTER EIGHT

They Strut

EXTRA–CURRICULAR ACTIVITIES

"Sometimes I have a hero (oops!, I mean heroine) dream. I dream right now I am going to get 'Miss Westfield' in the Beauty Contest. I also dream I am going to get the lead in the class play," writes Annette Boyd, a senior.

"Extracurricular activities are far more important than what happens in class," stoutly maintains one teacher. "The school would be better off without them," claims another. "What we should have is Monday for teachers only; Tuesday, Wednesday, and Thursday for classes only; and Friday for activities only," creatively suggests a third. Certainly, one of the characteristics of our educational system is the wide development of the extracurricular program. Here the students strut their stuff, evolving with vigor and enthusiasm their talents and dedication.

Extracurricular activities are voluntary activities carried on by the students outside the classroom. In practice, the line between the activity program and the classroom is quite fuzzy because activities often penetrate the classroom. Part of the activity program in the classroom is scheduled—students' programs normally include two minor subjects in order to give balance to the student's day. Sometimes these activity subjects involve participation in projects that require students to miss other classes. Dramatics class, for example, has for many years sponsored a Children's Theatre. The students write and enact a children's play and present it to elementary schools in the area. This is a rich experience for the students who produce it, and a delightful one for the students who see it. One play so involved the children in the audience that they shouted directions to the cast to straighten out the plot. "Which Witch Is Which?" was the title of the play, and the audience knew which one was the bad one, but the cast did not. However, these plays were presented so many times that the students involved missed several major-subject classes, much to the distress of their major-subject teachers.

Other activities also vie for classtime. The band goes on trips; team members of the various sports miss repeated afternoon classes for varsity games; classes go on field trips, often taking an entire day; student council meetings are held during school hours. Although these are the only official interruptions, in practice, many students manage to get excused from class frequently for other activities. Some students are so active in the extracurricular program that they seem just to check into their classes occasionally.

Sponsors, teachers who are responsible for an activity, sometimes are also responsible for some of this interference, becoming so involved with an activity that they bring it to the classroom. A teacher is more successful in recruiting participants from his classes for whatever activity he sponsors because communication is better there, and often class members are involved in the activity that concerns the sponsor. Classtime is apt to be generously contributed for completing work under these circumstances. I even had my classes involved in a Future Teacher's Conference one year when no member of my classes belonged to the organization. Many times activities so absorb the interest of the students that classwork is difficult if not impossible even though the students are there in body.

THE NATURE OF THE STRUT

In this school in 1960 the yearbook pictured thirty-eight clubs in which membership varied from fifty-eight in Tri-Hi-Y to four in the Debate Club. Some clubs are open to any who wish to join, and some are honoraries for which membership has to be earned. In addition to clubs, the sophomore, junior, and senior classes, the band, the athletic department, and the yearbook and newspaper provide areas of activity.

Small clubs come and go in our school, springing up because of some interest on the part of the students and dying down as the interest leaves. An example of this was my experience with the Modern Dance Club:

A student asked me to sponsor this club one year, assuring me that the fact that I knew nothing about modern dance was no problem. "We just have to have an adult in charge," she explained.

I agreed, signed notices for bulletins concerning the club, and attended their meetings. Ten or twelve girls were on the roll, but only six or eight usually attended. These were girls who had tried to make the chorus lines—the drum majorettes, the cheerleaders, and the pompon girls. Having failed, they organized an open club that would do much the same thing. Their president did most of the choreography, although all the girls contributed ideas along the way, and the meetings were practice sessions. The objective was to participate in the orientation program held in the fall to acquaint incoming sophomores with the various clubs. Their attendance at meetings was sporadic, their routines rather dull, and their accomplishment imperfect. However, their enthusiasm was great;

they believed in themselves and worked hard; they designed, bought, and made their own costumes, and most important of all, they presented their program. Once it was over, their need was satisfied, and the club faded out by the simple process of not calling any more meetings.

Psychology Club was a good example of the evolution of a club:

This club, although organized early in the history of the school, was inactive when I started teaching. Because of the interest of some of my students, I decided to reactivate it and called a meeting early in the fall. About twenty-five students responded. They elected officers, wrote a constitution, and planned a program for the year consisting of educational meetings on various psychological subjects. A professor from a nearby university came with a Skinner box and his rats for our first program, but only five students attended. In spite of valiant efforts from the officers, our serious programs had meager attendance, and we continued to struggle along until spring when the Psychodrama Troupe from the university was coming. This group was a busy group and required a small fee payment. Knowing a poor attendance would insult them, I recruited students from my classes by offering extra credit for attendance. Even with this, fewer than twenty-five attended. The officers and I then agreed that trying to promote serious programs for the club had little purpose, and we let the club die down.

When interest in the group revived the following fall, club activities began with an outdoor picnic. This was a big success with something like forty in attendance. Again they elected officers, and the officers planned a program for the year. The purpose of the club, according to its constitution, was to promote interest in psychology at the school, and on the basis of the experience of the previous year, we agreed, "We can best do this by having a good time." So we planned a social for each month. This time the attendance stayed high, and we had about fifty dues-paying members. The club, composed of both boys and girls, held socials which were mostly parties at people's houses, with picnics or outings during the good-weather months. That year we tried to raise some money to purchase some personality tests for use in psychology classes by sponsoring a school dance. The group worked hard on the decorations, publicity, and arrangements for the dance. We broke even financially, but the attendance did not justify the effort involved.

Membership increased the next year. In addition to continuing our socials, we sponsored a field trip to a mental hospital. The students became concerned with the conditions there, and we arranged to sponsor a ward. This involved monthly visits on Saturday afternoons at which time we took cigarettes, cookies, and some simple materials with which to entertain the patients.

The next year the club mushroomed and suddenly became *the* club to join. With 125 dues-paying members, sponsoring this group was like trying to drive a team of wild horses. This was too large a group to continue the simple parties that had been the basis of past success. Even though we moved the picnics to the park and they were fine, inside parties were a problem. An awareness of the danger of a school party getting wild prevents wise teachers from becoming involved in situations they cannot handle. "We will continue to have parties as long as they are decent," I cautioned them, and we did.

We had a Halloween party in an empty house that belonged to the family of one of the club officers. The house had been completely redecorated and was up for sale so that we had a great responsibility to protect the property. The committee decorated the entire house with imagination and skill. Students came in costumes and checked their shoes at the door to protect the floors. Although they had games, dancing, contests, and refreshments, the greatest entertainment of the evening was watching me try to keep out party crashers. This I achieved only by standing guard at the entrance; what else went on at the party was mostly up to the students, although another faculty member was in attendance. About eighty students came.

It was quite a party. Guitars in the basement, dancing on the main floor, and according to a rumor I heard afterwards, intercourse in the attic closet provided entertainment. I think one boy spiked his cokes, but he was a sophisticated drinker and just got quieter as the evening progressed. The students took excellent care of the property and left it as nice as we found it.

We had planned an Exam's End party at midterm. The students insisted it would not be wise to have it in a house, and so we arranged to use a recreation center in the area of the school. The day before the party, some of the officers came to me and advised me to cancel it. "There will be drinking," they warned. The compulsion to celebrate the end of exams with liquor seemed great, so I canceled the party. Although club activities continued for the remainder of the year, we had no other major social functions.

The next year we had a Halloween party at my house. The students warned me that the house would get torn up, but I argued that the best chance of having a decent party was at a teacher's house. The party was well attended, about two hundred drifting in and out during the evening. The weather was warm so we were able to extend the activities to the patio as well as the recreation room and the living room. The students were delightful, dancing in the patio and recreation room and playing games in the living room.

About eleven o'clock the doorbell rang, and I answered it to find a uniformed policeman standing there. The students gathered around to see what would happen.

"What do you want?" I asked.

"What's going on here?" he replied.

"We're having a party," I explained. "I am a teacher, and this is a group from my school."

"It's pretty noisy," he complained.

"It's only eleven o'clock," I pointed out. "The party will end at twelve, and this is Saturday night. There's nothing wrong going on here. These kids are having a good time."

The students departed at twelve as scheduled except for the ones on the clean-up committee, who left the house nicer than they found it. The next day the neighbors cleaned up beer cans from their lawns. I don't know whether some of the boys strewed them around for a joke or whether some of them were drinking in their cars during the party, but no one was obviously intoxicated, and I saw no drinking at all at the party.

On Monday the school was agog over the wild Psychology Club party. The fact that the policeman came was all it took. The story grew each time it was told even though I stoutly maintained that it was a great party and made no change in our party schedule.

The next one scheduled was at Christmastime. The students tried so hard. Although we made an effort to arrange it at school, no place in that large building was appropriate or available for a party, and it was again in my home. The students decorated, made refreshments, and planned activities for those who did not care to dance. Again, it was fun, but as the evening progressed I got the word from one of the students that I should move around. I went downstairs and found some beer cans which some college boys had brought in the basement door. I called one of the leaders aside and asked him if he could stop it. He said he thought he could. He got some of the boys to help him and they cleaned up what was there, throwing it out. He had to leave on an errand, and while he was gone, some more beer was sneaked in. This time when I found it, I had no choice. I turned off the music and sent the students home. "I'm sorry," I said, "but you can't drink at school functions. I would lose my job if I allowed you to."

They left in almost complete silence, and that was the end of Psychology Club parties. We continued meetings and service projects for the remainder of the year, but the spirit was gone. "It's time for a change," I told my principal the next fall, "and I think the new psychology teacher should sponsor the club." The principal agreed. The club took a new tack and is doing well, although it is a small club again.

In this school, the grade-level classes provide the basis of the most important school activities. The president of the senior class, for example, has more status than the president of the student council. The classes are rich because they collect dues which are voluntary in that no reprisals are possible if the dues aren't paid, but these dues are considered a measure of citizenship, and most students pay them. The money is used for proms, for graduation expenses, and for class gifts.

A high school prom is a fabulous event. Each year the elaboration escalates because it is necessary for each class to outdo the previous one. When I started teaching, prom decorations consisted of a crepe-paper canopy for the gym with an elaborate centerpiece. Through the years, the walls were decorated, and an elaborate entrance tunnel with chicken netting stuffed with small squares of crepe paper became a necessity. Then the cafeteria where refreshments were served had to be decorated. Then another class added decorations in the entrance to the school. Now the proms are held in the cafeteria, and the long halls are decorated. Proms cost somewhere around two thousand dollars. The last prom I attended was devoid of students by ten-thirty. The fifteen or twenty faculty couples had an expensive orchestra all to themselves with the enchanting decorations something of a mockery. The proms are held on Saturday nights, and the students have to leave the prom early in order to have any time at the nightclub which they visit afterwards.

Creating a prom is an important experience for the students who work on it. They spend long weeks in preparation; they learn much about the paper work of spending other people's money; they learn techniques of acquiring necessary materials; they learn to work together to achieve a common goal; they learn responsibility and perseverance; they learn to keep their poise when they are exhausted; they get acquainted with students they never would have known otherwise; and they get the thrill that comes from creative self-expression. No one who works on a prom, when the exhaustion is over, questions its value.

However, in a class of 742 students, about 50 of them do 90 percent of the work. A large number show up the night before the prom to do the actual construction that cannot be done ahead of time, but most of them are there for the fun and don't help much. The few who work, work so hard that they can scarcely stand on their feet when the actual event occurs. A general desire to hold the proms in a downtown hotel has been overruled by the board of education, which insists that proms must be held in the county. With no ballroom large enough to accommodate the group within those confines, the prom is kept in the schools.

The senior class play is much more successful as far as involving a large proportion of the class. The seniors do musical comedies which require a large cast, and the work crews swell the number involved to a large proportion. The experience of achieving these productions creates a vital unity in the class and gives individuals important opportunities for achievement. The Thespians also sponsor a play tournament in January, which consists of one-act plays produced by each of three classes.

THE BENEVOLENT EYE

Sponsoring clubs is a part of a teacher's responsibility, but in a school this size, the task is a voluntary one most of the time. Some teachers are eager to work on extracurricular activities, and this enables the ones not interested to be relatively free unless some task remains open. In this case, the principal assigns a teacher to the task whether the teacher especially wants to do it or not.

Younger teachers work hardest on the activity program. Eager for the less formal relationship possible between teachers and students in outside-of-classroom activity, these teachers find extracurricular activities add an important dimension to their teaching life. However, sponsoring a club is a thankless and difficult task, and since most of the older teachers have learned this, they are content to let the younger ones learn it for themselves.

Sponsoring a club is difficult in several ways. It is difficult because the sponsor is responsible for whatever action the club takes. The students are representing the school when they are participating in school activities outside the school, and the relationship between the school and the community is inherently involved. The students are aware of this in a vague kind of way, and usually they control themselves in this respect. When they don't, the sponsor may have a difficult or even impossible task on his hands.

Sponsoring a club is difficult because the teacher has to walk a tightrope on how much directing to do. Activities are opportunities for the students to learn from self-direction. Youth, however, often make mistakes when given free rein, and one never knows which mistakes are going to be good learning experiences and which ones are apt to be devastating. If a sponsor just sits back and lets the youngsters click along, they usually don't go very far. The students have too little experience to know what works and what doesn't, and if they have to learn everything for themselves, they are likely to make so many mistakes that the club will slow down and die. At the other extreme, if a teacher runs a club as he does a classroom, the club might just as well be another class. It loses its potential for teaching self-direction. The degree to which a teacher needs to direct a club also varies with the students involved. One year a club may be as inactive as a turtle in hibernation, and the sponsor needs to wake it up with a spring of ideas. Another year the same club may need the same sponsor to remain in the background because the students have their own ideas about what they want to do, and some of them are good. Although a club must have some successful experiences if it is going to survive, students also need some opportunities to learn from their mistakes. Thus it is a delicate line that the sponsor must constantly draw.

Sponsoring a club is difficult because it is time consuming. With many demands on his time, a teacher has difficulty finding the time to sponsor adequately. After-school meetings make a long day longer; evening meetings take up paper-grading and lesson-planning time as well as impinge on one's personal life; and weekend activities extend the working week to slave-labor hours. When large projects are reaching a climax, a teacher may need to use class-time to complete the project, and this interferes with what most teachers consider their primary responsibility—teaching classes. Sponsoring a club indeed takes time as well as energy.

Sponsoring a club is difficult because it holds the danger of strained relationships with students. One year the Psychology Club president, a delightful, vivacious, spoiled child, resented the fact that I was supposed to sign bulletin announcements regarding the club. She proceeded with considerable skill to get them through without my signature, causing me embarrassment and the club confusion by their nature at times. I finally succeeded in curbing her impulse, but the process required a great deal of effort. I also taught this girl in class, and some of the strain carried over into our classroom relationship.

Sponsoring a club is difficult because it poses the problem of maintaining professional attitudes in an informal atmosphere. One of the delights of sponsoring is the opportunity to relax with the youngsters and be one of them, in a sense. When such a relationship develops, frequent temptations to express honest opinions about fellow faculty members, school policy, and administrators arise. Such off-the-cuff confidences undermine professionalism and may come home to roost. Also club sponsorship creates a strain in one's relations with other faculty members at times. Teachers often resent any intrusion on their classtime. If a club activity interferes, they may aim this resentment at the faculty sponsor.

With all these difficulties, teachers continue to sponsor clubs because they offer important rewards in activities to the school, the teacher, and the students. The activity program is the seed of that precious bud of citizenship, school spirit. Because activities are voluntary, they give the student an opportunity to make a commitment to his community and to invest himself in making his school successful. This is, to the adolescent, the dawning of his commitment to his community, his country, and his world as an adult. The importance of activities in building this attitude was clearly demonstrated in the school one year:

> In a critical transition period for the new principal, the faculty took the first year to decide they didn't like him, and by the second year they had withdrawn to their classrooms where they did what was probably the best teaching of their lives. Beyond the classroom door they did virtually nothing. School spirit reached a low ebb by spring, and the situation in the school was critical. I could even feel the tension in the halls as I passed through them. Fortunately, the teachers became aware of what was happening and moved back into action before the crisis developed fully with the students, but it was too late to stop it entirely. Students developed the fashion of stealing the hall passes which had been provided by the new principal, and the entire faculty moving en masse could do nothing to stop them. We also had a massive senior skip day, which made national news. Both of these things, however, were mild compared with what might have happened, and the faculty became aware in a very deep sense of the importance of the activity program.

The most important value of sponsorship to the teacher is the delightful relationship with the students that activities provide. Here the youngsters reveal the best that is in them. Our youth today has a vitality, a forthrightness, and a dedication that is at its peak during the adolescent years, and being able to borrow this excitement of living by sharing these informal activities is a privilege. This relationship provides opportunity for understanding, which carries over into the more formal classroom situation, and helps the teacher in his relationship to all students. A teacher who has none of these informal relationships does not get as much out of teaching as one who does.

Teachers also sponsor clubs because they recognize that sponsorship is an official part of a teacher's load. If a principal asks a teacher to sponsor, the teacher has difficulty refusing. For a number of years I helped sponsor the junior class. The prom interfered seriously with my family responsibilities, and I asked to be relieved of the assignment. This was the only time my principal ever argued with me, and he tried to persuade me to continue. I explained my reasons and pointed out that I would continue with Psychology Club. Although he agreed on that basis, the pressure remained. A teacher is not doing his share in the school program unless he contributes to out-of-classroom responsibilities.

Some prestige accrues from sponsorship. The students admire the teachers whom they know best. Because of sponsorship, a teacher often achieves a high reputation that travels throughout the student body. Faculty members also respect fellow teachers who do a good job of sponsoring, although they are not likely to say much about it. Even administrators recognize the value of a good sponsor by preference in class load, teaching schedule, and assignment of other tasks.

Teachers also sponsor clubs because they realize that they are important to the students; and teachers do care about students, or they wouldn't be teaching. The best way to get a teacher to sponsor a club is to have a student or a group of students make the request. This is hard to refuse.

THE IMPACT OF THE STRUT

Activities are important to the students because they make them contributing members to the school community. "You ought to join at least one club," I used to advise my incoming sophomore homeroom. "You won't get as much out of high school if you don't." A student needs to contribute on a voluntary basis to his school if it is to be his school in the basic sense. Invariably the students who lack school spirit are the ones who have done nothing to make their school worthy of admiration, and conversely, the more a student works in school activities, the more he believes in his school. Classroom activities are the work of school life; extracurricular activities are the heart of school life.

Activities are important to students because they provide opportunities for achievement and self-realization. The high school years are years of self-exploration when the student is seeking a vision of his strength and skills as measured by the impersonal world. In the activity program he can find his niche and measure his size. He earns the status he achieves through accomplishments, and these achievements provide the basis of the self-confidence which will make him an adult. Classwork does this also, but activities inspire a child to reach further and to dare more with greater self-direction than the classroom can allow.

Because activities are voluntary, the practice of self-government within them is much more feasible than it is in the classroom, and this, too, is a valuable function of the activity program for youth. They can learn from their mistakes, and they can quit when they get tired and try again next year.

Activities are valuable because they give an outlet for the vital years of total commitment. High school students have not yet learned what they can't do, and because of this, they involve themselves in what they are doing more deeply than at any other stage of life. Never again will they spend so much on so little. From a rational point of view, spending two thousand dollars and all those hours of labor for a prom which lasts from 9:30 to 10:30 seems futile. From an emotional point of view, however, the creators of the prom are richer than they would have been with a hotel ballroom prom. They are people who enjoy being creative and take satisfaction in giving everything they have to finish what they start.

Activities are important because they give opportunity for interaction between students. Here a student is most likely to find friends among students with whom he has much in common. Boy meets girl; leaders learn to follow, too; and quiet ones are recognized when they walk the second mile. Because they are less formal and because they are voluntary, activities give sparkle to these relationships that classes seldom achieve.

Surely the teacher who claimed that activities are more important than classwork has some basis for her case. However, activities are no panacea for education, because they serve only a few. If the thirty-eight clubs averaged a membership of twenty-five, they would involve only one thousand students. Since many students join several clubs, this means that about a third of the students are involved to some extent. What about the other two-thirds? Why are they not active? An exploration of this question gives some possible reasons, but the fact isn't fully understood.

A large number of students do not participate in extracurricular activities because they do not feel at home in them. This program is an outgrowth of an upper-middle-class value system which does not fit the needs of lower-class students. For example:

> I hired one of my students to help with my housework one year. I chose her because she was the oldest of ten children and her father was a barber. She was a charming person—warm, delighted with an opportunity to make my home more beautiful, which though simple was more glamorous than hers. One of the senior-class officers was in her psychology class, and the class had discussed at length why more students did not help with the work of the prom.
>
> "We don't know what to do when we get there," one student declared, "so we hang around awhile and then leave."
>
> The day before the prom the entire class went down to work because the officer assured me that work was ready they could do. My housekeeping student enjoyed this and willingly did a share, even coming back that night to finish the project started. However, she never would have come otherwise because she would not have known the other students working nor what to do to make herself useful. She had long anticipated the prom, one of the highlights of her life. She brought a boy, though, whom she knew well and associated at the prom and afterward with a group of students who, like herself, would not have made the prom possible.

The striving inherent in the activity program is essentially an upper-middle-class value and is not a medium of expression and development for students with lower-class backgrounds.

Another group of students have no interest in the activity program because they are nonconformists. They prefer to seek their own way of life independent of the school program. These students may touch an activity now and then, but they are, in a sense, too sophisticated to involve themselves in chasing rainbows. This is particularly true of boys who seem during this adolescent phase to need to search for areas of success through individual enterprise rather than depend on a school club in which a sponsor sits around jacking up the group when it starts to skid.

A third reason some students do not participate is because they don't have time. Work permits are available at the age of sixteen, and many students have part-time jobs. These are important learning experiences for them, helping them sort out what they like and don't like for a lifetime vocation, but these do draw their interest away from the school and its activities. Many boys, in order to have their own cars, must work to keep them going and lose interest in school because of this. Some students need the money they earn to help their families and don't have much choice about working.

Transportation is also a problem in getting to and from the school for activities, although in this school the problem is not very great. Most students are of driving age and are generous with their families' cars, making it easy for the nondriver to hop a ride. Actually, most of them live within a 2-mile radius of the school and can walk if they have to. After-school activities, unless they are vigorous ones giving an opportunity for exercise, are not so popular as evening ones because no one feels like sitting after being in school all day. Most club meetings, except for brief business meetings or practice of some sort, are held at night.

Another reason why students do not participate in the activity program concerns the inadequacies of the program. The recent evaluation the school underwent rated the activity program quite high, and the school does have a good one. This program, however, is not uniformly good. Most clubs start out with great verve in the fall, slow down at Christmas, and stop by February. Only the excellent ones even continue meeting throughout the spring. Because students have little training in how to conduct meetings, a typical meeting is a wild affair with everyone talking at once. The fact that anything important gets said at all is surprising. People come and go constantly during meetings, adding to the confusion. A small proportion of what is planned materalizes, and what does materialize is often because a few conscientious students dig in and do it all. Clubs that are organized around an activity, like Gymkana or Chess Club, survive better than the ones that have to build their program as they go, but none of them function smoothly.

The activity program must depend on the faculty for its existence. Sponsoring a club is a very complex process, and somehow teacher training never seems to get to anything this practical. Some teachers apparently have inherent skill in this kind of endeavor, but most of them do not. Good sponsors are mostly those who have barged in and learned from experience what works and doesn't work in running a club.

The activity program is also inadequate because it is not a recreational program. Gymkana meetings are training sessions so that the club can perform somewhere sometimes. Chess Club meetings strive to improve the skill of the members so they can win a chess meet somewhere and enhance the glory of their school. Some students are not strivers. Rather than an organized program, they need areas of informal interaction in which they can relax and enjoy themselves with their fellow students.

ANIMAL FARM

One area of student activities is recognized as so important by the administration and faculty alike that it is allowed to impinge on the school day officially. This is the student council, the medium of student government. This is the one activity to which all students belong to some degree.

Student council members are elected in the homerooms. The homerooms are administrative devices for keeping attendance records and collecting and dispensing information for the functioning of the school. Student council meetings are reported to the homeroom, and any decisions from the students are made as part of homeroom business at the time these reports are made.

The student council meetings are held during classtime, representatives being excused from classes, both major and minor subjects. One of the student council responsibilities is to oversee the school activity program, which it does by granting charters for the various clubs. This process involves asking clubs to submit information which requires prodding to acquire. Since a sponsor's signature on a bulletin is sufficient to call a meeting, the clubs can meet without their charter. In spite of the fact that we made repeated efforts to provide the necessary information, to my knowledge Psychology Club never received a charter.

Student council publishes a student directory each year, an important contribution to the social life of the students because it includes telephone numbers. This seems to exhaust the resources of the student council, however, because by the time the officers and sponsors finish it, they are working at cross-purposes. Student council did sponsor a homecoming weekend to which alumni were not invited, and they are responsible for a big money-raising affair for which the various clubs present skits. Schoolwide activities sponsored by the student council on the whole seem to lack luster.

Several good reasons contribute to the ineffectiveness of the student council. The basic one is that the faculty fears a strong student council. They see no difference between the students running the school, and the students running themselves. They have no desire to be told by the student body what they should do.

A good demonstration of this attitude occurred when I walked into the school library one day.

> I found the librarian upset because a committee from the student council was coming to talk to her about restrictions on the use of the library.
>
> "What do they think they are?" she asked, "telling me how to run the library!"
>
> "I should think you would be glad they are concerned," I said. "I thought you were very unhappy about having to turn students away when you are overcrowded."
>
> After thinking it over, she decided to welcome them, and she did. The members of the committee became so incensed over the need when she explained the reasons why students were turned away that they wrote a letter to the board of education requesting an extension to the library. When this failed, the students went to their parents, and the PTA involved itself with this concern. Teachers depend on respect and authority to do their job. Their fear of a strong student council is not valid, but it is real.

A second reason the student council is weak is that the homerooms (about ninety) provide a cumbersome representative body. Just finding a space large enough for the group to meet is a problem, and constructive action with a group this size is hopeless. A student council executive committee was tried, but it wasn't representing anything and did nothing to solve the problem.

A third reason the student council is weak, and this is the most serious one, is that it does not represent the spectrum of social classes in the school. The basis of representation is the homeroom. The homeroom students are grouped alphabetically by grade-level classes and thus provide a random grouping of students in which they don't even know each other unless they happen to have common classes. In such a grouping, elected leaders are almost invariably chosen from upper-middle-class students. No one expects lower-class students, regardless of their leadership skill, to take the role of student council representative. Although the ones chosen are capable students, they represent a small portion of the school population culturewise, and they have no ability to sway or understand the needs of other class groups in the school society. Some powerful leaders exist in the lower social classes of the school, but they are never members of the student council. Communication both ways is nonexistent. Students don't know what is going on in the student government, and the student council has no finger on the pulse of most of the student body.

A fourth reason for the weakness of the student council is the inadequacy of its sponsorship. Teachers tend to be autocrats, and very few of them understand the democratic process. Administrators are even more so. In the ten years I taught, only one sponsor who worked with the student council knew what she was doing, and she assumed the responsibility only one semester because of the pressure of other tasks. The officers, although they often show great ability, are learning leadership techniques, and they make many errors. They need better-trained and better-oriented sponsors to help them with their problems.

The extracurricular activity program in the school adds an important element to the education of our youth. The students who reach for this training will form the committees of tomorrow's world, carrying the heart of living into adult life and making our society more effective than it would be if it were based only on the business of living. This program is not, however, the most important part of the school. The students who need help the most are least likely to participate in this program and must be reached in the classroom if their needs are to be met.

Thus one sees that strutting is not only fun, but taming as well. Here, however, the whip is gone, and the taming goes only as far as the student reaches.

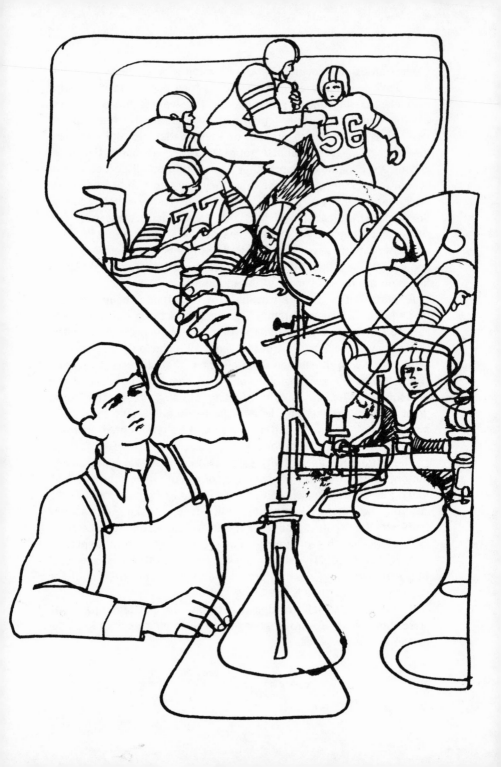

CHAPTER NINE

They Flee

ESCAPE TECHNIQUES

"The cool atmosphere of my chemistry room is partly responsible for my sporadic daydreaming. My mind seems to gradually drift away from the lecture until suddenly I find myself thinking about this week's football game or the things I plan to do during the coming holidays," writes Geoffrey Lane, a senior.

The cage door doesn't fit as tightly as some people think. When the tardy bell rings in the morning, one can see numerous students heading over the hill toward the nearby shopping plaza. The daily absence list presents even clearer evidence of skipping, i.e., being absent from school without the knowledge of parents. Out of a population of 2,600 students, somewhere between 200 and 300 students are absent daily, and most of these are skippers. During exams, when a doctor's excuse is required for an excused absence, this list drops to ten or fifteen names.

Skipping is prevalent for several reasons. If both parents are working, a student can stay home all day without his parents knowing it. Penalties for skipping are not very great, even when skippers are caught. At one time a student's grade was lowered one level each time he skipped. Parents, unwilling to have their children so heavily penalized, covered for them, and an aura of deceit permeated so many areas of adult-student relationships that the practice was abandoned. Now skipping is simply reported to the teacher who uses his own discretion about penalizing the student. A student's grade does suffer if he misses school because he loses contact with content development, and teachers seldom impose any further penalty other than a shocked look to indicate displeasure.

Most of the skipping occurs, however, because the school has no good system for checking absences. Each homeroom teacher is supposed to call the home of any student in his homeroom whose absence he suspects might be skipping. Since the teachers do not normally teach their homeroom pupils, they know very little about them and care less. Furthermore, they have no time other than their planning period to call parents, and that period often comes late in the day when that call seems ridiculous to parents and teachers alike.

When a student returns to school after an absence, he is supposed to bring a note from his parents describing the reason for absence. The homeroom teacher receives these notes and decides upon their validity. Because teachers are not handwriting experts, they cannot even question a poorly written, misspelled note. Often parents are less literate than their children, and such questioning could lead to cruel embarrassment. Most skippers write their own notes or get a friend to do it. Some teachers do not even bother to ask for a note. Although students are supposed to get the admission slip the homeroom teacher issues signed by each classroom teacher, students often go all day with no one catching such an omission.

Most students try skipping at least once in their school career just to see what it is like. Sometimes they stay home to do some special task for school they have delayed too long. Some students plan a rendezvous with friends and leave school for a lark. These reasons for skipping are fairly wholesome.

Most of the skipping, however, indicates the presence of deeper problems. In many instances skipping is a form of withdrawal from the life of the school. Such students are running away from problems with which they are unwilling to cope. A student may start to skip in order to avoid a test, and this practice can develop into a habit which will snowball to a record of eighty-five absences in a single school year. Such skippers find little constructive activity to fill their flight. They may stay glued to a TV for hours at a time, or they may wander the streets.

The most serious problem caused by skipping, however, is the effect it has on success in school. Regular attendance is a necessary precondition to success in school. Erratic attendance puts a student out of step with what is happening in his classes, and this in turn reduces his interest and effort. Just being there isn't enough to guarantee success, of course, but poor attendance is the first step toward failure and dropout for many students.

At the close of school one year, the principal called a faculty meeting to discuss means of controlling the skipping problem. After some discussion, one faculty member spoke up and said, "I think we should teach the ones who come and not worry about the rest. They are not important." No one challenged him. The incident was a weary end to a weary year.

Cutting classes is less prevalent. If a teacher takes a careful roll, checks his absences against the daily school list, and reports the discrepancies to the proper vice-principal, then absent students must account to the vice-principal. If a student has an unexcused absence, this is reported to the teacher who may refuse him makeup privileges and frown at him for his sin. This is enough, in most cases, to keep the student in class, and most class cutting occurs when the teacher doesn't check the roll. Skipping all day is so much simpler and is generally preferred.

THE GLASSY EYE

Most students come regularly to school and attend all their classes. Other forms of flight counter endless routine and boredom. As a teacher drones through a series of ideas that seem pointless and dull, that boy in the fifth seat in the third row begins to sag. His eyes become glazed, then heavy, and finally close altogether.

Some psychological dropouts spend most of their school hours sleeping. They have learned, like dogs confined in a house, to sleep their lives away. This is not as easy for boys as it is for dogs, but some of them have defied their enlarged cerebral hemispheres and spend most of their days oblivious to their surroundings.

Other students who sleep in class do so because they are tired. When a student seemed so consistently sleepy that I called him to task about it after one classtime, he explained that he worked at a local hamburger place from four until twelve o'clock each night and had to do his homework after that. In this case he had to work because of financial need in his family rather than a desire to pay for a car, and he was desperately trying to finish school. This situation is, however, rare.

Sometimes students need sleep because they have been studying late to do an overburdening amount of homework. Because teachers have no way of knowing what homework the students are given in other classes, students sometimes get a sudden rash of heavy assignments. If a teacher assigns a chapter one day to be ready the next, three other teachers might do the same thing for the same night, and the student is caught with more homework than he can reasonably do in one night. Most overload assignments, however, occur because teachers often do not realize how long it takes students to do a given task. Early in my teaching career I used a workbook coordinated with a textbook that had to be used in class since the students did not have individual copies of the text. I was astounded to discover that my best students could not complete in an hour a task that took me twenty minutes. Because study techniques are generally quite inefficient at the high school age, teachers can make unreasonable assignments without realizing it.

Pressure for grades to qualify for college forces some students to work more hours than they should.

Some students need sleep because they have stayed up late studying on special long-term projects. These assignments lend themselves easily to procrastination, and in these situations the burden is the student's own fault. This cause of fatigue occurs quite frequently, and many parents have unfairly condemned teachers for overloading their children because of these long-term projects.

Some students need sleep because they have been working hard on school activities, especially the proms and the plays which produce great demands on the students' time. The week before a prom and the month before the senior class play are periods when many students get the glassy eye. They are at school every night until midnight, and the excitement of the event further drains their reservoir of energy.

The athletic program is healthy from a fatigue standpoint because although the training program requires a large expenditure of energy, it encourages rather than interferes with sleep at night. The one exception is wrestling. During the wrestling season, some of the boys do excessive dieting to qualify for a lower-weight class. They are so tired they can't hold their heads up in class, and they are so hungry they can think of nothing but food.

Sleep is most common during fifth period, right after lunch. Many boys eat a double lunch with extra dessert, and no matter how much they try or care about what is going on in class, they cannot stay awake. The happiest year of my teaching career was the year I had fifth period free.

Some students need sleep because they have bad habits. They stay up late watching TV or just putter around inefficiently, putting off going to bed. A survey of morning routines of students made in connection with our study of habits over a number of years revealed, however, that many high school students have quite wholesome routines in regard not only to sleeping, but also to health habits in general.

Sleeping in class is fairly easy to control by the simple process of focusing attention on the sleeper. This amuses the class and is therefore all that is needed. Once the students ganged up on a fellow student who was in the habit of sleeping in my fifth-period class and decided they would slip out quietly when the bell rang so he would not awaken. He woke suddenly in the middle of the next class, and both classes had a laugh that spread throughout the school. Some teachers let students sleep because they prefer that to what the student might be doing to interrupt the class if he were awake.

Excessive sleeping in class, except for fifth period, is a good thermometer. If a teacher finds much sleeping, he might take a look—a look at the student and his needs, or a look at the lesson and its needs—because students usually prefer to flee in other ways and resort to sleep only when they need it.

UNDERGROUND ACTIVITY

A few students read the day away. Most of these are psychological dropouts who carry an endless series of paperback books dealing with cars or sex or science fiction. They slouch in their rear seats, pull out the book, and slip off to far horizons. No matter how cheap the fiction, eventually they run out of it and read something of value. Since science fiction can be creative and some value resides in almost anything one reads, I have felt that reading was one of the more preferable forms of flight and rarely interfered. Few good students have such lust for reading, but occasionally a good student will not be able to put a book down from class to class.

Good students are much more likely to flee by doing homework. Many students who spend hours on the activity program manage to maintain their grades by utilizing classtime for study. A teacher has difficulty telling whether John is taking notes on what is going on in class or writing an English theme. Even though utilization of classtime, much of which does not require full attention, may be commendable, a teacher finds a student poring over a history book most distracting when he is working hard at drawing a point from the class.

A more creative form of flight is doodling. One area in which progressive education has been obviously successful is in encouraging freedom in artistic expression. Most students today draw well, and many are quite skillful. Some psychological dropouts draw hour after hour and day after day. Their skill at drawing cars, cartoon-type characters, and grotesque figures is often impressive. While washing many an artistic masterpiece from my students' desks, I sigh and wish they'd use a sheet of paper so that it could be preserved. They aren't all talented, of course. Some just make aimless marks, and for them doodling is not much of a flight.

THE SOPHISTICATED FLIGHT

Once, when I was unexpectedly absent and had to whip up an emergency lesson plan a substitute could use, I asked the students to describe their favorite daydream. The seventy-four papers written by my students in response to this assignment reveal a panorama of this form of flight, making apparent its importance in the classroom.

A student writes:

> During the dull moments of my classes, when I should be paying attention, my mind often wanders to far off places. Although my dreams often vary in content, one stands out as the most vivid and most often thought of. It is also unusual, for instead of my dreaming of playing sports which you might expect, I dream of coaching them and, to add to this, I usually coach basketball in my dreams, a game which I have never been able to play for varsity.
>
> In my dreams, I am invariably coaching a small college team with but few players. The team has always been badly beaten in the past, and I have just begun to coach the team. The very first team that we face is our biggest rival which has yet to lose a game. The stands are always packed, although we are given no chance to win.
>
> But I, with a revolutionary new offense (concocted the night before) take my team out on the floor. In the locker room before the game I have given them a Knute Rockne-like pep talk. The game is close, but we eventually win the game in double-overtime. I am hoisted on the shoulders of my players and cut down the nets on the baskets as a victory symbol.
>
> After the game, I receive many congratulations and offers to coach all over the country. However, I refuse, saying that I am satisfied to work in a humble way for our good old Alma Mater.
>
> Just about this time, I am usually called on in class. I, awkwardly, ask the question to be repeated, and come back to reality, as hard as it may be.

"The thoughts of youth are long, long thoughts," and daydreaming serves some important functions during the adolescent period. Daydreams are stairsteps which students use to mount the stairway to their lives. The daydreams that give the greatest satisfaction are those that fit the pattern of one's life, embellished, of course, with hopes of achievement in excess of probability, but nevertheless related to one's abilities and interests. A youth tries out in his imagination the kinds of careers that are most likely to bring him satisfaction in his real life.

An example of a student's description of a vocational daydream follows:

> I often dream of being a career woman. I place myself in a large department store in New York City or sometimes in a small, exclusive dress shop in Valleytown. My job is buyer or fashion coordinator. I am assigned to an office with a large desk. There will always be fresh flowers on its corner. The carpet is deeply piled and a luxury to walk on. The walls are white, not stark white but sort of egg white. Modern art will adorn the walls. As I enter my office each morning my private secretary will already have the room well-lighted, just the right temperature, soft music playing and everything in order. Besides being outfitted for work the office will contain two large comfortable chairs with a table between. There will also be a full length mirror and dress form.
>
> My clothes will always form a complete ensemble in perfect taste. The style will be the latest from the best designers of Paris or Italy. My hair will always look perfect and my figure will be flawless. My job will allow me to travel around the world, meeting the most exciting people at each stop. I will have my own apartment furnished to my taste and I never have to call on my parents for aid.

Daydreams are also tension valves, letting off steam in a silent pose that permits return to pressured life with new vigor. An example of this comes from a male student:

> Usually my daydreams concern being somewhere where I am completely free, like the roads or a deserted beach. I am all alone and have no care or worries. Here I can do as I please. There are no laws or rules.
>
> I daydream most about this subject during the spring. It is usually then that I have grown quite bored

with school and yearn to be free. For the past few years
when school is out my cousin and I will drive up to
my uncle's "farm" in West Virginia and here all my
daydreams come true. My uncle lives in Terrysville but
takes trips to his place every now and then. He owns
50 acres which includes part of a lake and river. When
we go up after school we are completely independent
of one another. We go our own separate ways, do
what we like, when we like.

For two weeks this is heaven to me. I come back
completely refreshed and ready to meet the world
again. I don't daydream often but when I do it is
usually of the place in the mountains where I can be
myself for two weeks while I hunt, swim, fish, roam
and sit and do nothing.

For some, daydreams are a substitute for life itself, offering
temporary escape from problems in place of problem-solving activity. One student, skilled in such activity, describes her favorite daydream as follows:

My imagination runs not so far and wide as it runs
deep. In fact, I possess a sense of pretense that can
completely abandon reality.

My most prevailing daydreams know no present, only
a future. For a dream of the future holds more promise
and hope. Dreams of the present can come true through
the determination of the dreamer—a determination
shamefully I admit being void of. I lack ambition and
the stamina to withstand more than the minimum in
trials and tribulations that precede a dream come true.

There exists among my daydreams a prevailing
reoccurrence of marriage, a dream that is for the most
part realistic and practical. Two people who sip a coke
through one straw, dance together in perfect rhythm
(with the world as their ballroom), run hand in hand
through the marshes, lay side by side reading books,
and share life in its entirety. I see us living in our own
home, which I, to use rather simple adjectives, would
keep clean and neat. My mind often tarries on just the
exterior of our home. In fact, if this paper never sees a
concluding sentence, it is because I am decorating our
home with ideas that are wild, ingenious and abstract.
This is our castle, surrounded by trees. Within dwells
a couple whose love is never ending. The scenes of our
life together are, although clearly visible to me, quite

difficult to relate. We count the stars at night, travel,
blow kisses across the table, read, water-ski, listen to
our hi-fi, dance, argue occasionally, extend invitations
to our friends and relatives, smoke cigarettes, fight,
love, and fill each other's stockings at Christmas. He
brings me roses and lollipops. He grabs me and hugs
me and smothers me with kisses, an affection that is
returned. As the ideal wife, I'll cook, sew, serve green
lemonade on St. Patrick's Day, and be the Easter
Bunny at Easter for the man of my dreams. Another
dream, "The Prince Charming in my Life" I shall refrain
from further developing. Life is enduringly wonderful
to us. Our happiness together far outweighs the
natural perils of life and living. Eventually we enter
parenthood, shortly prior to which I quit working. We
are proud, understanding, and knowing parents raising
our first little boy (the first of four, two girls and two
boys).

Though this is, of course, not the end of my life, it is
the end of my dream. I failed to include details in the
actual writing of this dream, but it is, when visioned,
explicit in detail and specific situations.

This dream is not quite as realistic and promising as
it was; for the man of my dreams, whose path I had
crossed and together we had travelled as one, is no
more a part of my life. In utter fear and confusion, I
jumped the track. Although I hope to see this dream
eventually depart from its illusionative state, I am not
ready for its departure. The results would have been
permanent for ever and ever. And while dreams can
enter and exit at will, a person deeply involved with
another's life cannot.

Daydreams show quite clearly which students have creative imagination. Less than 10 percent could be classified as truly imaginative. The following example is the most unusual:

My daydream is probably very different from most
people's daydreams. In it, I am a different person, with
a different name, a different country, and a different
time. The time is not specific, but it is very long ago,
when man was just beginning to explore the possi-
bilities that his brain held. The country is the
mythological continent of Atlantis which may or may
not have existed. The northern part of this continent is
covered by a vast range of mountains and is inhabited
by tribes of barbaric people of the stone age.

Many beautiful valleys lie hidden in these mountains, and one of these is the Valley of the Purple Moon, the valley of my people. My name is the Black Tiger, given to me because a black tiger was the first creature I had successfully stalked, hunted, killed, and eaten. To the other people of the mountains, I am known as the Mammoth Boy of the Purple Moon. This is because my best friend is a great, brown mammoth, whom I have practically lived with all my life. Together we hunt, fish, and guard our valley from other tribes. To my people, I am a hero because many tribes would like to live in this valley, which is probably the most fertile in the whole section of the continent.

Most of the daydreams were almost stereotyped by the practical down-to-earth-goals they described. An example of this follows:

My favorite daydream is one on which I often ponder as it is one which I want very much to become realized. I often look into the future and picture myself in my middle age.

I see myself very happily married. My husband is a very fine man. He has few, if any bad habits, is gentle, kind, considerate, understanding and a good father.

My husband has an adequate income and I was able to quit work upon the birth of the first of my three children. My children are all normal, happy, healthy, intelligent, and well behaved. There are strong bonds between my husband and myself and they know that we are fair and just in our ways of discipline. My husband and I have few serious arguments, as we talk easily with each other and let each other know our ideas by discussing them among us.

I have many friends, and my family and others often get together for recreation. My family is able to make frequent small trips on weekends and holidays.

My husband and I each get along with our own and each other's family. My children are able to have close relationships with all of their grandparents and other relatives.

In short, my favorite daydream is that of having an ideal family and family life, and by doing my best in all my jobs at home, in my marriage, and in raising my children.

Many of the students' daydreams were more reminiscent than imaginative, as in the following example:

143

> My favorite daydream is reliving the wonderful time I
> had last August. I was working at Fern Creek Pool in
> Orlando, Florida. I spent 14 hours a day at the pool and
> enjoyed every minute of it. In the morning I taught
> swimming lessons to small children. Later I worked with
> children who were not so fortunate and had to learn
> in spite of having cerebral palsy. I spent the afternoon
> swimming or life guarding and the evenings taking
> Red Cross courses. When I wasn't doing anything else
> I would play hearts (cards) with the other life guards. It
> was so much fun except the pay stunk! I keep day-
> dreaming and remembering the good time I had down
> there. On weekends when I wasn't at the pool, my sister
> and I would go to Daytona Beach and spend the day.
> Those were really great times and now that there is only
> 3 months left of school I hope to go down there again
> and work next summer.

Most of the daydreams had little emphasis on material desires.
Less than 10 percent of the daydreams described concerned
material gains, and even these were modest except for one girl who
visioned millions. The following example is typical of those dreams
primarily focused on the material world:

> My daydreams are mostly about money and boys. I
> think instead of classifying it as money, I should say the
> things in life and the position. The daydream that
> occurs most often is with my ambition. When I'm older
> I intend to start to work toward being a whiskey sales-
> woman. This type of job pays very good money, up to
> $400, so of course I dream of what I'm to do with the
> money. When it starts to roll in I'm going to get an
> efficiency apartment in one of the new apartment
> projects. I'm going to live alone because I'm used to it
> and living with other people gets on my nerves. The
> next thing to come will be the furniture which will be the
> very best of Italian Provincial that I can find. This is a
> very important aspect of my dream. Another thing that
> is also important to me is clothes which I will buy
> between furniture payments. Of course I have to have
> a car. Some people dream about a big fancy Cadillac,
> but all I would like is a small MG-Td. Of course I have to
> eat and drink. My refrigerator will be stocked with
> nothing but steak, potatoes, lettuce, tomatoes, and
> avocados, To drink will be gin and Tom Collin. One

thing I forgot in the furniture account is that I want rugs
on all the floors and floor to ceiling drapes.
   P.S. All these things may seem very trivial but they're
very important.

The same percent that dreamed of material things dreamed of
freedom. An interesting example of this type of dream follows:

I feel that if I must choose a favorite daydream I would
have to choose between the daydreams I have during
my school day. My most typical dream is that of being
free. In English I happen to sit next to the window
from which I can see the tops of the trees and the sky.
I catch myself staring out the window admiring the wide
open sky which has no limits. It reveals a spacious
nothingness with nothing to worry about, a will of going
anywhere it pleases at any time it pleases, and no
chance of falling to earth and being associated with the
ever-present anxieties of the stereotyped earth people.
I also catch myself staring at the leaves of the tops
of trees. I think of them hanging on for dear life trying
not to become detached from their mother's arms.
At the top of the tree they have no worries. They are
supplied with food, air and ever-present care from the
mother plant. I feel they fear falling to the hard earth
where they will be torn away from their food, care, and
free clean air. On the ground they can acquire no food,
must fight for clean air, and eventually as all
human beings die.

One-fourth of the daydreams concerned love and marriage. Two-
fifths of the boys dreamed about sports. One-fifth of the daydreams
concerned the student's immediate life, as the following example:

My favorite daydream for the last two weeks has been
about the play. At first I was only going to sing and
try out for a minor part. A friend persuaded me to sign
up for a major part. Right now I could almost kiss
him. Because I did that, I was one of twelve boys who
got a script for the part of Freddy.
   Last night were the tryouts and I believe that I did
my best. Ever since the singing tryouts last week, I have
frequently caught myself daydreaming about the
thing. The most common one is the one about the
announcement of characters Friday (tomorrow) in fifth

period. I have visualized the calling of "Freddy—
James Green" quite a few times.

I guess the reason for this is that I have never done
anything to be really proud of in my three years here. I
am just the average student who comes, goes to
classes, does his homework, and goes to bed. This is
my first and probably my last time to do something
that will make my senior, as well as sophomore and
junior years, a success. This may seem childish to some
people, but not to me. I am dead serious. I do realize,
however, that I probably will not get the part. I was
going against some very good actors. Time will tell.

I also dreamed about my tryout all last week. I
dreamed of doing good (which is on the right track
anyway) and winning the praise of Mr. Jerome right
there. Of course I didn't win the praise of anyone, but
neither did any of the others.

That daydream did come true partially, however. I
did do the best possible for me. I was handicapped
somewhat for lack of acting experience, but as I have
previously said, time will tell. The one thing I am
thinking now as I close is, Will my daydream come true?

Ten percent of the daydreams described as favorites concerned
traveling and these were mostly girls' dreams. One of these follows:

My favorite daydream is not formed from misty mental
images which float through the mind like thin cloud
vapors. It comes to me instead sharp, vivid and clear as
I flip the pages of a travel magazine or peruse the
pages of a geography book. I have a desire to see the
world.

I can almost feel the salt spray when it blows onto
the deck of a great ocean liner as the ship glides along
the furrowed sea enroute to Europe. The white cliffs
loom ahead days later near Dover. I walk along the
glassy streets of London in a thick drizzle; I talk for a
minute with the woman selling flowers on a corner.
Big Ben chimes the hour and I continue to ramble.
Swish goes the red cape of the matador as he entices
the bull in the dusty arena below me. The crowd shouts
in a tongue now familiar to me. I sit down to rest my
weary feet at a sidewalk cafe. While sampling a French
delicacy, I can study the black skeleton of the Eiffel
Tower as it is silhouetted against a pastel sky. Gazing
down into the smelly water as it swishes past the sides
of the gondola, I can see the reflection of the houses

*nearby. After this brief ride, I stroll into the giant square
and tame pigeons rush at me suspecting a handout.
I shut the book and settle back in the chair; the photo-
graphs from the pages persist, graphic and intense
even while I continue my daydream with eyes closed.*

Four girls dreamed about service to mankind:

*The streets are crowded, and the noise of taxicabs
blowing their horns fills the air. A baby cries of hunger,
and a mother screams in anger. This is a sample of
the atmosphere that I find myself. I find myself talking
to a family which has just come over to this country,
telling a story to a group of children, or just plain
listening to the problems of a drug addict.
It is a hard daydream to describe since every time I
think about it it's different.
Whether in Harlem, Chicago's East Side, or in
Washington, that's where I want to be if I can be of
some assistance. This need to help someone else has
always been with me. Perhaps my daydream is an
outlet which will satisfy my wants.*

Only eight of the papers could be classified as conquering hero
daydreams, although many of them dealt with success:

*Cheers and applause greet my jazz group as we walk on
stage at Newport. We've only been recording for a year
but we are the hottest group around. We have a new
style which is similar to the "new thing" but more
aggressive. We have provoked a new style which is
catching on all over the country. The group consists of a
saxophonist, a drummer, a pianist, and a bassist.
Complete silence hovers over the thousands as we begin
to play. Piercing and soft sounds are projected above
novel rhythms. After the first number there is
thunderous applause. Cries of "More! More!" work
their way through the cheers.
Soon, we become the most popular group and
empathetic group in jazz. We have bookings up to three
years in advance. Plans for a tour of Europe and Asia
have already been made. We have a contract with
Impulse for four records a year. The records we've made
already have sold close to a million copies each. New
groups spring up trying to copy us but it is an impossible feat. Old groups try to master our sound but are
unable to. Critics have nothing but praise for us and we*

win every jazz poll in existence. Our group is on top
to stay, and never to be conquered or equalled.

Only two of the daydreams were examples of suffering hero daydreams. Both of these follow:

A daydream is usually a sequence of imagined events
that are created by the dreamer (who is not asleep) in
order to delight or satisfy. When I daydream, though I
begin by conscious creation of people and places, I
find that unconsciously this dream is always replaced
by the same vision. How this apparently uncontrolled
image comes about, I do not know. But I will describe
it here, realizing that it is not a "daydream." There is a
long gray stretch of beach. A storm is either coming
or just leaving and the ocean is dark and choppy. The
sky is the most dramatic element, full of dark and
light patches and clouds of the most fantastic shapes.
There is a high cold wind and the sky, or perhaps the
air, is a strange murky green-yellow. I am sitting on a
rock, a few yards out from the beach, in the water.
I am not wearing shoes. I am thinking about a friend
that I love dearly and who has hurt me very much. The
friend may be different, but it is always a real situation
and the love is very great and the hurt is very deep.
I am very much aware of the wildness of the sea
and sky.

I do not think I actually have a favorite daydream.
I usually think of the matters at hand and then imagine
what could happen in the future because of the
present situation. But there is one thing that I do
imaginatively think about often. It is not a favorite
because I really hate to think it but the thought usually
occurs. Sadly enough my daydream is about a boy.
He is a boy I at one time seriously dated but we ended
our relationship for various sensible reasons with
mutual understanding. When I daydream about him it
is nearly always the same situation. He is in an awful
automobile accident and is seriously injured. No
one else is ever involved or hurt. He is taken to the
hospital and within a short time he dies, never regain-
ing consciousness since the impact. He never seems
to be physically injured, yet he always dies. Sometimes
my daydream has gone as far as to the funeral parlor
where he is laid out for viewing. His relatives and
our friends are there but no one ever says a word. My

*dream has never gone further than that because then
I am shocked back into reality.*

Daydreams may reveal much about the dreamer's background,
such as follows:

*When I am doing one of my many household chores I
find myself thinking and pondering over a favorite
subject of mine and that is the new Jerusalem. Although
the beauty and glory of it is beyond my human comprehension or understanding, I still wonder about it. The
streets will be of a pure, clear gold. That will be the
cheapest thing there. The gates will be made of pearls;
and the mansions will be made of twelve types of
diamonds. There the "beast from the wild shall be led
by a child" and the "lion shall lay down by the lamb."
No tears will be known for God shall wipe away all
tears from the eyes. There will be "no sickness no
sorrow" and "no troubles" at all. There will be no children crying from hunger or from fear or because
they miss their parents because they did not love them
anymore. In the new Jerusalem, there will be no
billboards advertising cigarettes or beer or the prevent-
ing of highway accidents. The people there will have
a heavenly appearance on their faces and everyone
shall be known to each other. The songs that will be
sung will be praises to the Lord. They will sing of his
wonderful love to all mankind. This is my
favorite daydream.*

Two students denied that they daydream at all. One wrote:

*I can't remember ever daydreaming. I used to "think"
about one thing or another and I still do. Of my
thinking, the most prominent one is that of wanting to
have to really work to the grindstone for whatever I
want. I don't ever want to have things just "go my way"
—that's too easy. Everytime I think of something I
want, or want to do or become, I always manage to
think of the roughest way to that goal. I wouldn't call
this a daydream though because it's fairly realistic.*

"By their dreams you shall know them," and these daydreams
reveal much about the nature of today's youth. Any objective
attempt to generalize on the basis of these daydreams seems seriously to miss the mark. Their value lies in their subjectivity. Much

149

of their significance becomes apparent in relation to a knowledge of the individual characteristics and background of the students who write them. Needless to say, dreams also lead to a deeper understanding of the students' needs, goals, and background. Approximately one-third of the students did not do the assignment. Whether this was because they did not wish to share such inner thoughts, or whether they resisted this assignment for the same reasons they do others is impossible to say, but this is not an unusual proportion to fail to do a particular assignment.

My first impression on reading these papers was awe at their beauty. Each one seemed a separate jewel revealing something meaningful about the inner life of the student who was writing. The assignment seemed to touch a chord that was significant to the students, and they not only were carefully done in regard to neatness, punctuation, and other mechanics of writing but also were quite genuine. Whatever these students are or may become, they aspire to that which is best in life. No need for violence, hate, fear, or anger appears in their dreams. They yearn for love, adventure, freedom, and security. Their dreams are beautiful.

My second impression was to note the maturity of these youngsters. Their daydreams are so sensible it saddens me. Only seventeen or eighteen years old, these students seem almost to have had no youth. Although this quality appears in other ways, it is most vividly portrayed through their daydreams.

My third impression was that, generally speaking, these students are not very creative. A few of them were delightfully imaginative, but most of them were not. Their dreams are practical and usually well within the realm of what they may achieve rather than glorious meanderings into the impossible or flight into fantasy.

While students sit and daydream in the schoolroom, they are thinking important thoughts most of the time, sometimes more important than what is going on in the classroom. A final example of a daydream must close this section:

> I would like, more than anything else, to be a true
> woman in every respect. One who is intelligent and yet
> ignorant; free and yet dependent; a mystery and yet
> understood; influential but dominated; striking but not
> beautiful; helping but also helped; and most of all,
> loving and loved. I believe that man's purposes in life

are many but not varied; they are all related in some
way to goodness. He should create beauty, give assist-
ance, seek love, enjoy laughter, encourage under-
standing, and further peace. He should develop to their
fullest his mental abilities, spiritual beliefs, and
physical strength. But most important he should never
stop giving for, selfish as this may sound, it is only
through giving that we receive.
This is my philosophy of life and all my daydreams,
whether I am in East Berlin fighting for my freedom
or in Harlem trying to help a dope addict want to stop,
picture me as my ideal. I know that I will never
fulfill this ideal but I will always work towards it
realizing my compensation that when I do fail I will still
have my dream.

All students need to escape some of the time from the humdrum of classes. Some students need to escape all the time. In between lies the vast majority of students who try to focus on classwork activity, but find their attention slipping in spite of their good intentions. They are much more likely to interact with other students than to use the forms of flight described above, but classroom control being what it is, they must draw from these methods rather frequently. Many times these activities are more valuable to the students than what is going on in class, and when the classwork picks up momentum, the student returns.

Thus, with their own techniques, the students resist the taming. This is good. Our youth are more than animals, after all. They are young men and women in the process of becoming, and their power of resistance is also important.

CHAPTER TEN

The Cage Door Opens

CONCLUSION

"When the weather starts getting warm, I sit in class and think about my experiences at the beach. I feel the sand and the surf and all the excitement of the gang having a great time. I just can't wait till school is out," writes Gordon Paul, a senior.

My last day of teaching was bright and cool for June. Although my senior classes had left a week before for graduation, I had a busy morning. I wished my sophomore homeroom a happy summer and commiserated with them because they would not be able to make bulletin boards for me their senior year. I fought a valiant battle with the annual attendance report and won, at least temporarily. I locked the keys to my car in the trunk while loading some of the accumulated paraphernalia of ten years of teaching and knew I was stranded at school until my husband could rescue me with his duplicate late in the day. On my desk I found a sentimental note of farewell from a homeroom student too shy to say good-bye, and I helped the library finish its painstaking inventory in time to report to my spot in the hall as the zero hour approached.

The principal had assigned each teacher who was free of classroom responsibilities that hour to patrol the halls the last half hour and keep students in their classrooms until the release bell rang. Just as I reached my spot in the middle of B wing, an attractive, middle-aged woman approached.

"I am Mrs. Parsons," she introduced herself, "Adele's mother."

"I am delighted to meet you," I responded, "Your daughter has been so much fun to teach this year. I am sure you realize she is quite talented."

"Yes, but . . . ," she started to reply.

"I beg your pardon," I apologized, as I spotted a student strolling up the hall. I broke away from her and accosted the student.

"Where are you supposed to be?" I asked.

"In biology," he replied.

"Well, go on back," I ordered. "You are supposed to stay in your classroom till the bell rings."

"I have to go to the bathroom," he argued.

"You can wait," I insisted. "It won't be long."

Reluctantly he turned back toward his classroom, and I returned to Mrs. Parsons.

"I'm sorry," I said, "you were saying?"

"It's not Adele I have come to see you about," she replied. "It's James. You know Adele has been going with him recently, and I wanted to find out whether or not he is college material."

154

"Yes, I have been much interested in their romance," I said. "Adele was so pleased when he finally asked her to the graduation dance. James is a remarkable boy, and I admire her taste."

"But how intelligent is he?" she asked worriedly.

"Excuse me," I mumbled as I rushed to stop two other students meandering through the hall. They went back placidly enough at my insistence, and I returned, collecting my thoughts as I went, to the waiting parent.

"Intelligence means many things," I explained to her. "James certainly is not brilliant in the way Adele is. Few people are, and this is one of the biggest adjustments she must make in life. James, in his way, is a most unusual person. An intelligence test score for him could be most misleading because his ability is in relating to people rather than ideas, and he doesn't work very hard on scholarship."

"But can he do college work?" she persisted.

"Just a moment," I said. By now the noises in the hall were reverberating. Students would peek in the hall, see me, and retreat while some were popping in the door from the court. When I sent two boys back for the second time, I wasn't quite sure they would go, but finally the hall was clear and I returned to the parent. The clock pointed to five minutes until the closing bell, and I somewhat frantically said, "I don't know whether James can do college work or not. He hasn't been much of a student in high school, but. . . ."

Just then the two boys came down the hall for the third time. I turned to them in my firmest voice and said, "I told you to stay in your classroom until the bell!"

They broke and ran straight past me.

All the frustrations of ten years of inadequacy seemed to well inside me, and without even realizing what I was doing, I turned and tore down the hall after them, calling in my loudest, lowest tone, "Who do you think you are!"

Although fast for my age, I was no match for them in speed. When they reached the main hall, another teacher tried to stop them. They split, one running one way and the other, the other way. She stood helpless, not knowing which way to go and was almost as angry as I.

At this point, the bell rang, releasing hundreds of happy kids, singing and shouting and throwing papers and worn-out notebooks around. Refusing to give up, I tore up the steps to the front exit of B wing, hoping to catch at least one of them when they went outside. It was useless, of course, and I returned, stopping to exchange caustic comments with my cohort.

Suddenly I remembered the parent whom I had so rudely left standing, a witness to my lack of dignity. I reluctantly returned, wondering what I could possibly say to her. Much to my relief, she was gone. Then I started to laugh. What a fitting ending for my teaching career—a blaze of violence and indignity and futility without reason or perspective. How else could one who cares so much depart?

The boys I chased will be back next fall, up on the second floor among the juniors. They will be a little taller, a little heavier set, perhaps, and more subtle in their pranks. With tanned faces and with new notebooks filled with fresh paper tucked under their arms, they will greet their friends joyfully. When they enter their classrooms, they will be on their good behavior, at least for that first magic week of school. They will carefully observe their teachers to see what lies ahead for them that year.

As I write these closing words, I wonder who will be at my desk—someone young and full of dreams and ideals, I hope, with stamina and courage and some fear, perhaps. He might have read this book, and if he has, I hope this view of the taming helps a little in his great adventure as he calls his first class to order.